LEGAL ISSUES JOURNAL

Volume 4 Issue 1 January 2016

www.uklsa.co.uk/law-review

Legal Issues is an international journal managed and published by the UK Law Students' Association (UKLSA). The Journal publishes fine research in all fields of law on the basis of its contribution to the society, originality, interdisciplinary interest, and quality. *Legal Issues* also provides important news and interpretation on changes in the legal world and coming trends affecting law, lawyers, and society. The Journal has two primary aims. First, to facilitate a forum for the sharing of knowledge, news, and trends concerning the application of the law throughout the globe and for further development in all fields of law. Second, to ensure the dissemination of fine accessible work to the public throughout the world.

ISBN-13: 978-1522795582
ISBN-10: 1522795588
ISSN 2050-005X (Online)

The United Kingdom Law Students' Association

http://www.uklsa.co.uk

Divisions

Academic Division
Publications Division
Equalities Division
Careers Division

Schools Division

Contents

Companies of Past and Present: Lessons from the East India Company on the Use and Regulation of Private Forces Today

Katerina Galai[†]

This article considers issues of international legal classification in the historical and contemporary context of the use of private military by states and non-governmental organisations. There is more to these questions than contemporary practices can reveal, so this enquiry begins with a historical approach, tracing the lineages of private security through centuries. Particular focus will be on the status and composition of the colonial army of the English East India Company, drawing parallels with the current private military company (PMC) regulation. This article raises questions about the customary notions of 'public' and 'private' in order to draw attention to the changing nature of military norms and to build a stronger case for regulation. Building upon British colonial activities in India, the article demonstrates the importance of maintaining control and revising codification of new irregular military forces.

Keywords: Army of the East India Company, codification of irregular military forces, Private Military Companies, public and private violence.

1. Introduction and Overview

In the 1990s there were fifty military personnel for every one contractor, now the ratio is ten to one.[1] 'Coupled with the current general trend towards

[†] School of Law, Politics and Sociology, University of Sussex.

globalisation and privatisation, and the failures of the international community to respond to each and every massive humanitarian crisis effectively, it is little wonder that we are witnessing substantial growth in private security today.'[2]

This article begins by scrutinising the relationship between the state and the military, which highlights the importance of understanding the historical variability of the normative approaches to public and private military power in order to regulate contemporary PMCs, and to codify new types of private forces under international law.

Then, we analyse the governmental construct of the British Empire in India with a particular focus on state administration, financial, and legal structures that were deeply involved in military ideas and practices. To address regulatory constraints, it is not enough merely to identify the leading contemporary norm. We also need to understand what form of governance it applies to, as the normative aspects are only indicative of broader shifts, revealing little on their own. [3]

Next, this article analyses the army of the East India Company through the lens of power and legitimacy, and examines its composition, role within the Empire, and its relationship with the sovereign in order to determine if such colonial army should be considered a public or a private force. Finally, the article puts forward some normative arguments as to why the Crown preferred to outsource, which allowed for inherently stately functions, such as local administration and the military, to be governed by a private trading organisation for over a century. The historical example of the British colonial army highlights the importance of regulation, mirroring the current issue with PMC classification.

The so-called 'public' monopoly on armed forces in the context of the nineteenth-century imperial European state did not derive from within state borders or even from within Europe. Imperialism added a new, legally undefined, type of military force to the existing choice of mercenaries and citizens – access to imperial troops.[4] In the era when states were consciously moving away from using foreign mercenaries, this article suggests that it was because of the lack of laws and customary norms that colonial armies became a viable and popular alternative.

---

[1] P. W. Singer, *Corporate Warriors: The Rise of the Privatized Military Industry* (Cornell University Press, 2004).

[2] K. O'Brien, 'What should and what should not be Regulated?' in S. Chesterman and C. Lehnard (ed), *From Mercenaries to Market. The Rise and Regulation of Private Military Companies* (Oxford: OUP, 2007), 33.

[3] T. Barkawi, 'State and Armed Force in International Context' in A. Colas and B. Mabee (eds.), *Mercenaries, Pirates, Bandits and Empires. Private Violence in Historical Context* (London: Hurst & Company, 2010), 50–51.

[4] P. Owens, 'Distinctions, Distinctions. *Public* and *Private* Force?' in Colas and Mabee (ed.), 25–26.

The article concludes by deliberating the concepts of 'public' and 'private' force through Weber's definition of state in the context of contemporary PMC regulation issues, and raise questions about the importance of classification and codification of irregular forces under national and international laws.

2. British East India Company

While most accounts use the post-Westphalian nation-state as the starting point for the norm against the use of mercenaries, my analysis builds upon historical examples of different forms of governance in order to trace transformations of irregular military forces in each of those constructs.

What constitutes a 'legitimate' military? A legitimate military for absolute monarchies was the emergence of a standing army — the salaried professional army of Spain, Sweden, and Prussia. In republican thought it is a citizen militia of Italian city-states, advocated by Machiavelli's idealised Roman republic. The nation-state of revolutionary France gave birth to a national army, while the army of the British Empire was predominantly composed of colonial subjects.

Following the Peace of Westphalia in 1648 and the rise of the modern State, the trend to use mercenaries was fading away making strategic space for standing armies. The Napoleonic wars of the end of the eighteenth century marked the pinnacle of this transition. Given the lack of military organisation of the non-European states and the absence of any legal limitations on a state's ability to commence a war, it was inevitable that European colonial empires expanded through the conquest of large parts of Asia and Africa.[5]

'Empires brought with them a need for specialised troops in permanent readiness for colonial duty. Of all these the most remarkable was the East India Company's army.'[6] Founded in 1600, the English East India Company[7] was run by a Court of twenty-four directors. With its key focus on competitive trade, by the first half of the eighteenth century the Company achieved a status of a respectable commercial body, connected with City of London banking

---

[5] A. Anghie, 'Finding the Peripheries: Sovereignty and Colonialism in Nineteenth-Century International Law' (1999) 40(1) Harvard International Law Journal 51.

[6] V. G. Kiernan, *Colonial Empires and Armies 1815–1960* (Stroud: Sutton Publishing, 1998), 23.

[7] Literature of the East India Company: C. H. Philips, *The East India Company 1784-1834* (Manchester: Manchester University Press, 1961); B. Gardner, *The East India Company: a History* (London: Granada Publishing Limited, 1971); H. V. Bowen, *The Business of Empire: the East India Company and Imperial Britain, 1756-1833* (Cambridge: CUP, 2006); J. Keay, *The Honourable Company. A History of the English East India Company* (London: Harper Collins, 1993).

and the Stock Exchange.[8] Originally, the East India Company had a determinedly pacifist outlook and was mainly preoccupied with commerce.[9] Later, the Anglo-French struggles of early- to mid-eighteenth century were an important factor to Company's territorial expansion and assertion of governing power in India.[10]

With the power of the Mughal dynasty[11] dominating throughout the sixteenth and the seventeenth centuries, the Indian Empire was the second greatest power in the East, following that of Peking.[12] Whether the accession to power of the British in India was made possible by the factions in the Mughal rule[13], the Hindu-Muslim tensions[14] or the emergence of a new order in eighteenth-century India,[15] the British lost an opportunity to create a much stronger form of sovereignty that originated from trade and effective organisation of local resources. Furthermore, there was no Indian nation *per se*, and no sentiment of national unity which made it possible for external powers to interject and impose their rule, simultaneously offering a new form of unity. 'There was no political discourse in eighteenth-century India to construe resistance to the foreigners as a national war for the defence of the country.'[16] In the absence of centralisation, numerous forces fought for dominance over different parts of India. Moreover, these forces often preferred British rule to the authority of one another.[17] The needs of Indian rulers for cash and troops met the British ambitions to play a political role as military commanders and bankers to the State.[18]

When Bengal became a British-ruled province it granted the Company's servants possession of vast territories, authority over about twenty million people, as well as access to three million pound sterling in revenues.[19] What was extraordinary about this colonial example was the way the Company achieved its sovereign status. The Company was penetrating beneath the surface by building up its strength not on commerce alone. It used the local

---

[8] D. K. Fieldhouse, *The Colonial Empires: a Comparative Survey from the Eighteenth Century* (London: Weidenfeld and Nicolson, 1966), 140.
[9] M. Ferro, *Colonization: a Global History* (London: Routledge, 1997), 55.
[10] See Fieldhouse, 166–167.
[11] Also known as 'Mogul'.
[12] See Fieldhouse, 162.
[13] Ibid.
[14] P. Spear, *India. A Modern History* (New York: University of Michigan Press, 1961), 186.
[15] P. J. Marshall (ed): *The Oxford History of the British Empire. The Eighteenth Century* (Oxford: OUP, 1998), 493; See Fieldhouse, 163.
[16] R. K. Ray, 'Indian Society and the Establishment of British Supremacy, 1765-1818' in Marshall, 519.
[17] See Spear, 228; The Marathas preferred British rule to Muslim; the Rajputs, British suzerainty to Maratha; and the Muslims, British rule to Hindu.
[18] See Marshall, 497.
[19] See Marshall, 492.

resources–popular, administrative and military–to establish its rule and then to expand it, while retaining the formal control of the territory.[20] It also held control over military resources. However, those forces were not under direct rule of the British Empire. These were privately managed, locally sourced and funded by the profits of the Company, taxes raised through Indian administrative systems, or, bribes received directly from Indian aristocrats.[21]

3. British Indian State

Who was governing and what was being governed? In the south, the British occupation created a new state; whereas in Bengal, the Company operated within a state that was already formed.[22] It dealt directly with the local power,[23] respecting the local customs and focusing on economic rather than cultural imperialism. 'Indian princes, who contributed men and money to the Imperial effort, were treated as valuable allies—to be protected, if necessary, against the protests of their own subjects.'[24] Sovereign status came to the British Indian state in 1765 (also known as the Company Bahadur). The treaty between Robert Clive[25] and Emperor Mir Jafar delimited the frontiers in a parallel administration, while the parliamentary enquiries at home served the legitimising purpose of enforcing responsibility on the governors.[26] 'Government by committee, or Council, was one of the many legacies of its commercial origins that survived the East India Company's transformation into a ruling power.'[27] Interests of administrative service were predominantly private which reflected in the way the trade was regulated, or more accurately, dominated by the Company and its servants.[28]

Just as the Indian states were built on the taxation levied from the cultivators of the land, the British Empire in India was built on the same premise.[29] The dynamic private sector bound the Indians and the British through active trade and voluntary subordination of wealthy Indian merchants to the Europeans in exchange for security and stable commerce.

---

[20] See Fieldhouse, 164.

[21] Indians who wished to hire the Company's troops had to pay the Company, as well as to reward their officers privately.

[22] See Marshall, 502.

[23] See Spear, 194.

[24] See Washbrook, 402.

[25] Also known as Clive of India; he was a British officer who established the military and political supremacy of the East India Company in Bengal.

[26] See Spear, 203.

[27] See Ray, 513.

[28] Ibid., 515.

[29] See Marshall, 504.

Legitimacy had to be established in order to claim power over the new territories, and that would not be possible without the introduction of the rule of the law in the English Presidencies, following the India Act of 1784. [30] The British became administrators of Indian law, presiding over courts in which issues of rights to land and distribution of revenue were decided[31]. However, in military and administrative practice, just like in trade, the local traditions had to be respected if the Company was to stand a chance of becoming the new sovereign. The common denominator amongst administrative, financial and legal functions was the ever-growing role and presence of the military apparatus, rooted at the core of the state and the society.[32]

4. THE ARMY

While gradually becoming the central infrastructure of the British Indian state, and a regional military force that had no match, the army of the East India Company had a rather complex constitution full of contradiction and inequality. The historical composition of the army—the way it was raised and organised—created ambiguity around its status.

Should the colonial army be considered public or private? The significance of this distinction lies in the contemporary claim that post-Westphalian states chose to move away from mercenaries and alternative types of military force to a national standing army. Furthermore, historical classification issues highlight parallels applicable to current PMC regulation.

As the army was directly controlled by a private organisation—the East India Company—it is especially important to examine the notions of public and private in the contemporary military context. The unequal application of sovereignty between the Metropole and the Empire also highlights the gap, potentially suggesting the exclusion of colonial subjects from the public, civic, as well as military spheres.

The eighteenth century marked a shift in the Great Power struggles from European issues to markets and territories that ranged across the globe.[33] To compete in this new global arena and to establish supremacy in India, Britain had to exceed Dutch and French military and commercial efforts on the subcontinent. Administration of vast overseas territories was expensive and

---

[30] The India Act was then implemented in India after 1786 by the reforming Governor-General Lord Cornwallis; see Ray, 520–521.

[31] See Marshall, 504.

[32] From the mid-1820s the government of India maintained 'sixteen European regiments of the line as well as a permanent standing army of 170 sepoy regiments, totalling 235,000 men.' See Washbrook, 402.

[33] P. Kennedy, *The Rise and Fall of the Great Powers. Economic Change and Military Conflict from 1500-2000* (London: Fontana Press, 1989), 195.

impractical unless 'use was made, wherever possible, of existing political structures and resources.'[34]

In order to save costs and preserve already low numbers of the British soldiers, the Company chose to obtain its military manpower from local sources.[35] The indigenous population, although lacking training and the unity of a professional army, could be had at a much lower price than British soldiers. Although the French had piloted the sepoy[36] conscription following the compulsory enlistment structure at home, Britain soon realised the great advantages local armies could bring. Following the French example, the British raised their own sepoy forces, grouping these into battalions in Bengal and Madras by the late 1750s.[37]

Unlike the French, who used coercion as a method of enlistment, the British offered voluntary service, which was a much more attractive alternative for the sepoys. As the voluntary service was an accepted norm by this time for free-born Britons, conscription was hardly ever formally employed to subject peoples across the empire.[38] To make the enlistment contract between the soldier and the Company more lasting, as well as to attract recruits and to purchase their quiescence during service, British policymakers deployed material incentives.[39]

Until the European invasions, Indian military culture was predominantly feudal, with private mercenaries serving a different warlord based on pay and opportunity. French and British imperialists introduced an effective mechanism that gave the sepoys a military framework and a sense of job security, while simultaneously ensuring a constant supply of military manpower for the Empire. This European pseudo-standing army created a real sentiment of fraternity by offering the sepoys discipline, uniforms, and a regular pay that also guaranteed their loyalty to the Company. Furthermore, the use of more advanced fire arms made the sepoys stronger and more effective than their local opposition.[40] Equality ended there, however, as no sepoy, however long his tenure, could ever rise above the rank of a 'native officer'.[41]

While most armies and some navies still contained elements of international 'service' mercenary nobility,[42] standing armies prevailed across

---

[34] D. Held and A. McGrew et al (ed), *Global Transformations. Politics, Economics and Culture* (Cambridge: Polity, 1999), 41.

[35] See Kiernan, 16.

[36] Sepoys comes from the Persian word *sipahi*, meaning 'soldier'; see Omissi, 3.

[37] Ibid.

[38] See Kiernan, 16.

[39] See Omissi, 48.

[40] See Spear, 191.

[41] See Kiernan, 26.

[42] Mann (1993), 420.

European nation-states and empires. However, there was one more little known — yet extraordinary — element to the East India Company army that puts in question its status as a public force. The Company's army was formed from the sepoy regiments and the Royal Army. Although controlled by a national command, the Company's European troops consisted of large non-national European numbers. In 1781, the British East India Company hired two Hanoverian regiments.[43] These German auxiliary troops were hired out by a prince to the British, amongst other imperial powers, under a subsidy treaty stipulating the number of troops, the term of service, the geographical area, and the missions they could be used for, in return for financial and political benefits.[44] The presence of auxiliary troops, although regulated, brings a mercenary facet to the composition of the East India Company army.

5. Normative Angle: Why Did the Crown Choose to Outsource?

With the crystallisation of the concept of a nation-state, standing armies flourished and grew in strength and size. The new political relationship between citizens and state meant that citizens were perceived as representatives of their home country. As citizen armies became the new norm, states also began to pass neutrality laws, which prohibited their citizens' enlistment in foreign armies. The rise of this institution of neutrality was also driven by state rulers' interest in controlling their power over society.[45] In the latter half of the nineteenth century, according to Thompson, the great powers preferred to reserve the national population for their own uses, as the main military focus on the continent turned to building mass national armies. [46] For Barkawi, this combination of the institution of neutrality and the imperatives of nation-state building, on Thompson's account, meant that mercenarism declined as an institution.[47] According to Owens,

> [T]he full import of the mobilisation of imperial soldiers by both trading companies and national armies, incredibly significant in terms of numbers and 'control' for nineteenth

---

[43] C. Tzoref-Ashkenazi, 'German Auxiliary Troops in British and Dutch East India Companies' in N. Arielli, and B. Collins (ed), *Transnational Soldiers: Foreign Military Enlistment in the Modern Era* (Basingstoke: Palgrave. Macmillan, 2013), 32–33.
[44] See Tzoref-Ashkenazi, 32; also see Kiernan, 16.
[45] See Singer, 31.
[46] J. E. Thompson, *Mercenaries, Pirates and Sovereigns. State-Building and Extraterritorial Violence in Early Modern Europe* (Chichester: Princeton University Press, 1994), 96.
[47] See Barkawi, 38.

> century world politics, is passed over in a largely 'normative' explanations for the decline and delegitimisation of the 'private military market' in this period.[48]

The same argument is actively promoted by Percy;[49] however, the example of the greatest imperial army questions the validity of this trend.

The context of colonial history alludes to a broader geo-political conditionality that played a significant role in the new military configuration. This conditionality arises from the availability of disposable cost-effective colonial resources. In addition, the brutal and legally dubious — nature of colonialism makes it problematic to consider the move away from mercenaries to be a norm driven by morality.

While national sovereignty[50] became an established notion in Europe, power and legitimacy of overseas empires could be instilled in other apparatuses than just the state. Empires followed a different logic whereby the state was not the sole institution that possessed military power and the tools of legitimacy. The East India Company is a vivid example where the main state functions had been outsourced to an offshore organisation that had little direction or constraint from the ruling governmental body at home. The East India Company ascended to power through trade, ingenious use of local resources, and the backing of the government at home. It established the rule of the British Empire through Company methods and carried it out through Company's servants. It had discovered and secured the jewel that the Crown was long to cherish, yet not, in fact, control.

In the time when 'war and the military were central to state leadership and foreign policy',[51] the British Empire was, in essence, outsourcing the sovereignty, administrative, and military authority to a trading organisation. Why did the British state not show any interest in assuming responsibility over the Indian territories?

Several explanations can be found. The British Parliament had little knowledge of India and the population and, while it may seem unimportant on the grand scheme of colonialism, it was exactly the knowledge and uninterruption of the local culture that granted the Company its prevalent authority. To a great extent, the Company had a firm hold on the local infrastructures and was able to build connections that were fruitful not only for Company servants, but for the Empire as well. Hence, there was no advantage to interfering with the successful management of affairs of the

---

[48] See Owens, 27.

[49] S. Percy, *Mercenaries. The History of a Norm in International Relations* (Oxford: OUP, 2007), 121–122.

[50] Here meant also as territorial sovereignty.

[51] M. Mann, *The Sources of Social Power: Volume 2, The Rise of Classes and Nation-States, 1760-1914*, (Cambridge: CUP, 1993), 413.

Company. At the same time, however, unceasing disapproval of the Company servants' behaviour suggested that urgent action was needed to regulate various aspects of British activity in India. 'To assist with this process, two committees of inquiry were established in the House of Commons to review the recent history and current state of the Company's affairs.'[52]

On one hand, resistance from the Company was a significant obstacle to Crown's assertion of power and authority in India. Company servants were making fortunes of private arrangements with the local princes and merchants, and their reluctance to give it up to the British government was evident and robust. On the other hand, ministers in the Metropole wanted to avoid imperial responsibilities. The legal status of the Company's possessions had not been clarified, and while numerous assertions of the state's right to the Indian revenues had been made by ministers, these had not been supported in law or statute.[53]

Negative perception of colonialism was another prominent norm and it had both political and ethical roots. For example, there was a strong reluctance from the British state to compromise its virtue. In addition, Armitage suggests that 'the attributed character of the Second British Empire – as an empire founded on military conquest, racial subjection, economic exploitation and territorial expansion – rendered it incompatible with metropolitan norms of liberty, equality and the rule of law, and demanded that the Empire be exoticised and further differentiated from domestic history.'[54] This logic supports the ethical vision as to why the governance and the military functions of the Crown were outsourced to a private company.

These elements contributed to the structure of colonial relationship that was handled at arm's length, removing direct responsibility from the Crown by creating a buffer of supposed legitimacy between the morally advanced Britain and the 'backward' colonial regime. The tactic of outsourcing military functions to a non-governmental body is something states use to this day in order to bypass the rules and sanctions of international law, therefore transforming the East India Company 'from an historical curiosity into a highly relevant case study.'[55]

6. STATE MONOPOLY OF FORCE

Though there was little doubt that the British military had moved away from the use of foreign, private, or irregular forces, the Indian Army was often

[52] See Bowen, 537.

[53] Ibid.

[54] D. Armitage, *The Ideological Origins of the British Empire* (Cambridge: CUP, 2000), 3.

[55] *The Economist*, 17 December 2011 at http://www.economist.com/node/21541753.

referred to as mercenary. Formed of colonial subjects and two German auxiliary regiments, the enlisted soldiers fought for pay —not to selflessly defend the Raj.[56]

At what point does this disjointing take place? The two concepts, mercenaries and colonial army, were purposefully separated by the layers of imperial and Orientalist logic to manage British public opinion at home whilst successfully pursuing colonial goals abroad. This same approach is often deployed today by states using PMCs as part of their foreign policy.

We will now examine some of the key aspects of a nation-state in terms of customary international law in the context of contemporary world order. To what extent does the description fit the reality? Does the international legal system that was built on the premise of such states continues to serve a good purpose? To narrow this question, we focus on the notions of state responsibility, the decline of Westphalian sovereignty and dilution of state power by the new emerging non-state actors, all in the context of the use of force.

According to Max Weber, 'a society is organised as a state where there is a successful monopolisation of the exercise of legitimate violence. 'The State' is simply whatever agency it is that discharges that function.'[57] While there is no doubt that the British Empire was a fully formed State in Weberian terms, the Crown did not hold the monopoly of violence. The governmental construct of British India was a classic case of what has been called 'sub-imperialism', that is, of the dominance of local interests over metropolitan ones.[58] The source of authority was determined by men actually in India, as opposed to Company directors in London, or even more so, the Parliament. This is a question of responsibility.

7. State Responsibility

Should these colonial troops be considered a public force or a private force outsourced by the Empire? Either choice opens a debate on accountability and ownership of the military force. Quasi-state-owned, these troops existed under the imperial rule and the extended sovereign capacity of the hegemon. The empire had broadened the scope of its power to incorporate new territories and the resources that came with it. The British Empire could, therefore, be perceived to have retained the formal control of the use of force within the

---

[56] See Omissi, 47.

[57] R. Geuss, *History and Illusion in Politics* (Cambridge: CUP, 2001), 15.

[58] See Marshall, 498–499.

territory.[59] Under such interpretation, the modern state can also be said to retain formal control of the use of force, as it can allow military and security firms to operate from its territory and mobilise them to pursue own ends.[60]

However, accountability lies with the Company for two key reasons. India was ruled directly by a small number of Company's servants heavily reliant on the local political and administrative structures and a locally raised Indian army. It was also controlled indirectly, through Indian princes, treaties, troops and resident advisers (the source of *de facto* authority). In effect, until the sovereign power was officially transferred to the Crown in 1858, the British Indian army, alongside the administration of the British India itself was fully governed by a private company.

Unfortunately, Weber's definition makes no distinctions between 'public' and 'private' violence, leaving it open for states to interpret the boundaries of legitimacy. Equally, these notions have evolved over time, and the divide between public and private is a modern phenomenon that has taken on a variety of meanings.[61] Commonly associated with the state and centralised governmental remit, 'public', in a military context, ought to represent the force that is controlled by the sovereign. What if the sovereign chooses to use 'a mostly foreign and private force for one purpose (CIA covert operations), a foreign and public force (colonial armies, foreign legions), and a domestic and private one for yet some other (US private contractors in Iraq)'[62]? Another basic feature of the notion of a public monopoly of force is the assumption that only citizens can form the armed forces, with the citizenship rules governed by each individual state. However countries like the US, the UK and France have legal mechanisms that enable foreign citizens to serve in their militaries.[63] Are states in a position to choose different configurations based on cost, resource availability, and other factors, as long as there is appropriate control mechanism in place for their responsibility to be invoked?

The mere fact that a state conducts its policies through proxies should not render international law inapplicable.[64] The rationale behind the attribution of authority, codified in International Law Commission Article 8[65], is to ensure

---

[59] N. White and S. MacLeod, 'EU Operations and Private Military Contractors: Issues of Corporate and Institutional Responsibility' (2008) 19 (5) The European Journal of International Law 969.
[60] See Owens, 27.
[61] See Avant, 23.
[62] See Barkawi, 50–51.
[63] Ibid., 47.
[64] C. Lehnard, 'Private Military Companies and State Responsibility' in Chesterman and Lehnard (eds), 143–144.
[65] ILC Article 8, Conduct directed or controlled by a State: 'The conduct of a person or group of persons shall be considered an act of a State under international law if the person or group of persons is in fact acting on the instructions of, or under the direction or control of, that State in carrying out the conduct'.

that a state does not evade its responsibility by transferring its functions to a private entity. Whether one accepts the view that states retain the monopoly of force today, or that the privatisation of violence is challenging that monopoly, much of the current debate is constrained by a Eurocentric image of the territorial state in which force is organised behind the sovereign borders.[66]

7.1. Decline of Sovereignty

By its nature, private force upsets conventional understandings of state monopoly of force. This theory is a prerequisite for a nation-state, which arguably has been slowly eroding since the end of the Cold War.[67] In practice, contemporary manifestation of a state monopoly of force is also limited, as we see PMCs being widely used both for humanitarian and belligerent goals. Furthermore, the decline of the Westphalian notion of state sovereignty must be taken into account when looking for an appropriate function for private force in conflict resolution and post-conflict reconstruction.

According to White and MacLeod, the traditional Westphalian narrative of states as the sole subjects of international law prevails, rendering corporations ostensibly devoid of international legal constraint.[68] But does the Westphalian nation-state construct prevail? Looking back at history, a wide range of differing governmental constructs can be identified, the nation-state being only one of many. Perhaps it is worth a critical examination of the contemporary state system and comparing it to the definition and practice of what the nation-state stood for in its origins. Perhaps the state system we have today has moved along and transformed into a new format, whereby states are no longer strictly bound by borders (e.g., Shengen, EU, Commonwealth, CIS), but rather grouped by economic and political interests, happy to trade in a portion of their sovereignty in exchange for another kind of security. So, is it possible that the conservative view of international law no longer fits this new form of governance and the idea of state monopoly of violence becomes more diluted amongst the actors who have access to security recourses?

---

[66] F. Halliday, *Rethinking International Relations* (Vancouver: University of British Columbia Press, 1994), 78–79.

[67] S. McFate, *The Modern Mercenary. Private Armies and what they mean for the World Order* (Oxford: OUP, 2014), 74.

[68] See White and MacLeod, 968.

7.2. Dilution of State Control

State monopoly of force is one of the widely accepted Weberian concepts that helps to define the boundaries of legitimate violence. Further to the narrative of public and private violence, there is an important feature to the contemporary monopoly of power — it no longer belongs to states alone. While it is true that states continue to be the main owners and users of military power, the growing number of operational[69] and advocacy[70] NGOs, multinational corporations[71] and global political players such as the UN and NATO, has changed the political and legal dynamic by adding new actors to the international arena. It is important also to mention terrorist organisations, who, not only claim authority, but also change the political landscape by resorting to asymmetric warfare. This is yet another non-state actor that controls the means of power and violence, typically in parallel to a formal government.[72]

'In coping with the changing role of the PMCs, at least in the short term, a repositioning of the public-private parameters that determine state responsibility for private conduct might be the most viable solution.'[73] The changing role of PMCs cannot be viewed in isolation. The exponential growth of private military activity is directly linked to the current globalised state system. Whether failing or co-dependent, states no longer uphold the same extent of sovereignty as they did throughout the most part of the twentieth century. Moreover, they are overarched by global legal and political institutions and undercut by multinational corporations, shifting states further from the Westphalian concept of monolithic entity that comprises all governmental functions behind the sovereign borders. To that end Sean McFate speaks of Neomedievalism[74], a term coined by Hedley Bull. Neomedievalism suggests an alternative to a Westphalian state system that is characterised by technological unification of the world, the regional integration of states, the rise of transnational organisations, the disintegration of states, and the restoration of private international violence.[75] All of these elements suggest a shift from a Westphalian state system and highlight the decline of territorial sovereignty.

---

[69] For example, Medecins sans Frontieres, Oxfam and the Red Cross; see McFate, 79–80.

[70] Advocacy NGOs that hired PMCs include, but are not limited to: Save the Children, CARE, CARITAS, GOAL, IRC, and Worldvision. McFate, *Supra,* 80.

[71] Such as ExxonMobil and Walmart.

[72] More on the new actors on the international arena see McFate, 77–89.

[73] See Lehnard, 156.

[74] Neomedievalism is a metaphor loosely based on the world order of the European high Middle Ages, but it does not portend a literal return to the medieval period. An alternative to the Wetphalian system researched by Philip Cerny, Mark Duffield, Jorg Friedrichs, Stephen Kobrin and others.

[75] See McFate, 75.

Finally, the growing presence of the private military industry today indicates that the market for force is shifting, marking a decline of state monopoly of force.

8. NOTIONS OF PUBLIC AND PRIVATE

With some of the power and legitimacy elements considered on the side of the state, we turn to the military aspect to scrutinise the notions of private and public violence. In the absence of clear regulation, the line between public and private tend to be blurred. The example of the British Indian army is a testament to this ongoing issue.

Colonial armies fostered the spread of the empires and made their existence sustainable, providing a legitimate and accessible substitute for foreign mercenaries. While the Western hemisphere was consciously building national armies and moving away from mercenaries, colonial troops could easily be deployed due to an existent legal loophole. The areas where charter companies took on military functions fell outside the established order of the European state system.[76]

A similar issue arises today with PMCs operating in an environment regulated by a number of international and domestic legal provisions, often incomplete and conflicting. Several international organisations have attempted to bring clarity and order into the complex and fast evolving realm of international security. To this point, according to the Global Policy Forum, UN efforts to regulate the private security industry have been largely inadequate, mainly because the nations that are most likely to use PMCs have not ratified the Convention.[77] A tragic example that demonstrates this was the genocide in Rwanda. Executive Outcomes approached Kofi Annan at the outbreak of Rwandan atrocities in 1994. Ironically, the UN was firmly set against using a private military company to address the crisis. The inability mobilise public forces in a timely manner, and the reluctance to defer to a PMC resulted in over 800,000 casualties, which exceeds the combined number of victims in Iraq and Afghanistan.[78]

Even when international law tries to accommodate the changing world order, its power of enforcement is conditional. It can only be applied if the states subscribe to regulation. An evolving exception to this rule is the

---

[76] See Singer, 35.
[77] Global Policy Forum, PMSCs & the UN at <https://www.globalpolicy.org/pmscs/50225-pmscs-a-the-un.html>.
[78] See McFate, 38.

International Criminal Court that, in some cases, may investigate and try citizens of states that have not signed and ratified the Rome Statute.[79]

Doswald-Beck argues that the most significant change from the 1949 Geneva Convention, applicable to the use of mercenaries, is the blurring of the lines between the regular armed forces and other armed groups.[80] While Protocol Additional I to the Fourth Geneva Convention of 1977 provides the most widely accepted international definition of a mercenary[81], some states have not endorsed it and are instead governed by the previous Convention where the definition of combatant, and therefore prisoner of war, is more inclusive.

For example, the United States is not party to Protocol Additional I and is bound by a combatant and prisoner of war requirements outlined in the Third Geneva Convention, allowing for private troops to be considered combatants. To a certain extent, states can pick and choose their participation in the Conventions depending on the criteria, therefore leaving enough room for political interpretation to execute operations like Blackwater.

'Some forms of violence are *made* public and others are *made* private through historically varying ways of organising and justifying force.'[82] The lack of coherent international regulation and codification of private military forces creates room for interpretation for those upholding power and legitimacy. Furthermore, in the absence of a clear and widely accepted separation between public and private violence, and, if the nuances of private violence are not explicitly codified, powerful states can bend the rules of interpretation to their advantage on a case by case basis.

During the Coalition Provisional Authority (CPA) administration in Iraq,[83] a legal framework was established stipulating the regulation of PMC activities:

> 'In accordance with international law, the CPA, Coalition Forces and the military and civil personnel accompanying them, are not subjects to local law or the jurisdiction of local courts. With regard to criminal, civil, administrative or other

[79] Ibid., 78; on ICC jurisdiction over citizens of non-parties see J. Elsea, *International Criminal Court: Overview and Selected Legal Issues* (Congressional Research Service, 2002), 25–26.

[80] L. Doswald-Beck, 'PMCs under International Humanitarian Law' in Chesterman and Lehnard, 120.

[81] The Protocol Additional to the Geneva Conventions of 12 August 1949, relating to the Protection of Victims of International Armed Conflicts, Protocol I, Article 47, June 1977; Some countries, including the United States do not support The Protocol.

[82] See Owens, 32.

[83] 21 April 2003 – 28 June 2004.

> legal process, they will remain subject to the exclusive jurisdiction of the State contributing them to the Coalition.'[84]

The reference to international law does not seem to bear any judicial or practical meaning as it was not mentioned at all during the proceedings of the Blackwater Trial,[85] making a clear statement about the civilian status of PMC contractors and disabling the vehicle of International Humanitarian Law. Such legal configuration puts the blame on the company and the contractors, entirely bypassing international law and leaving the hiring state free from responsibility.

Another attempt for regulation of the PMCs has been put forward by the International Committee of the Red Cross. At the fourth meeting on the 'Swiss Initiative' in September 2008, the Montreux Document was finalised and adopted by consensus of the participating governments.[86] The Montreux Document is an intergovernmental document intended to promote respect for international humanitarian law and human rights law whenever PMCs are present in armed conflicts.[87] While insisting that PMCs do not operate in a legal vacuum, the Montreux Document seeks no binding authority from the participating states or the non-state actors using the private security services. It elaborates on different agreements (interstate, belonging to international organisations, national laws, etc.[88]) that stipulate state behaviour in relation to the PMCs. The issue arises from the lack of clarity on the legal prevalence in the private security sector. As most international legal regulations function in conjunction with one another, the lack of clear legal guidance on this matter is nothing novel. What is of interest, however, is the state-oriented approach to a network-based private field of activity.

The multitude of regulations creates a 'legal vacuum'[89] as well as hinders standardisation of the sector. Many of these companies are no longer mercenaries in legal terms; they are registered and operating openly under a certain license. However, the remit of their legitimate activities is still under question and the liability issue remains unresolved.

---

[84] Office of the Administrator of the Coalition Provisional Authority Baghdad, Iraq; Public Notice regarding the Status of Coalition, Foreign Liaison and Contractor Personnel, 26 June 2003.

[85] J. Stewart, 'Inside the Blackwater Trial,' Conference paper presented at the Institute for Global Law and Policy, Harvard Law School, June 2015.

[86] Federal Department of Foreign Affairs, Section for International Humanitarian Law at http://www.eda.admin.ch/psc

[87] The Montreux Document, 31.

[88] Ibid., 20, 24.

[89] T. Catan, 'Private Armies March into a Legal Vacuum', *Financial Times*, 10 February 2005; P. W. Singer, 'War, Profits and the Vacuum of Law: Privatized military Firms and International Law' (2004) 42 (2) Columbia Journal of Transnational Law, 521–550.

9. THE IMPORTANCE OF CODIFICATION

The term 'mercenary' has been used to describe everything from individuals killing for hire, to troops raised by one country working for another, to private security companies (PSC) providing military services to their own country.[90]

Looking at historical examples of nation-states and empires, a shift away from mercenaries cannot be viewed in isolation from the terminology that differentiates the nuances of various types of military power.

For example, some historical accounts[91] view the use of colonial armies merely as the sovereign's choice of military power. However, a deeper differentiation between 'public' and 'private' challenges such a view. While Britain may have ceased hiring private mercenary companies for its own national army after the Crimean War[92], it fielded hundreds of thousands of foreign soldiers before and after 1854 in the form of colonial armies[93] (not forgetting the recruitment of German auxiliary troops who acted as part of the royal army). So, in reality there may not have been a conscious shift away from the use of mercenary or private forces; the lack of regulation and the novelty of colonial armies was a lucrative ground for raising a cost-effective mass army through the legitimate use of non-national forces.

Contemporary private military forces fall into a similar category, as the lack of comprehensive regulation and clear codification makes it impossible for PMCs to operate without facing significant criticism, often being labelled immoral and illegitimate. 'Unless a regulatory framework places home states PMCs under the same level of scrutiny – both in the public eye and in government – as national soldiers, then those companies can still be criticised for threatening citizens' control over the use of force.'[94]

The only reasonable argument as to why they may not be breaking international law is simply because PMCs are not currently defined or bound by it. 'The difficulty is that moral objections to private force reveal there are very clear lines of descent from mercenaries through the PMCs and to the private security companies of today. While PMCs can, and have, worked hard to avoid the ethical objections about killing for money, they run into the same objections about tyranny as their predecessors.'[95] Although mercenaries are defined in the Geneva Conventions, there is no specific mention of PMCs in International Humanitarian Law treaties or in the customary international law.

The distinction between individuals acting as mercenaries and those working for companies under a certain contractual obligation is important for

---

[90] See Avant, 22.

[91] See Fieldhouse, *supra*, and Kiernan, *supra*, and White and MacLeod, *supra*.

[92] See Percy, 148.

[93] See Barkawi, 40.

[94] S. Percy, 'Morality and Regulation' in Chesterman and Lehnard, 27.

[95] Ibid., 28.

attributing responsibility and defining legality. If an individual (or a group of individuals) chooses to resort to belligerent activities without an overarching authority of a state (national army, police) or a licensed company (PMC), and those activities are not conducted in self-defence or in the context of civil war, this individual ought to be classified as a mercenary and his activities should be deemed illegal under national and international laws (international humanitarian law, human rights law, international criminal law).

While the purpose of this article is not to define the boundaries of legality of non-state military actors, it draws upon historical example of colonial armies in order to demonstrate the criticality of making those distinctions.

Similar to current peacekeeping operations fielding the multitude of resources supplied by private military and security companies, British colonialism in India provided context for a new, unclassified type of military force. Thompson calls it 'extraterritorial violence',[96] referring to foreign military manpower, as well as the existence of private military forces of various kinds such as those employed by the great trading companies of the early period of European expansion.

10. Conclusion

To conclude, private security takes various forms. Whether it is a colonial power, auxiliary troops incorporated into a state army, or a private military company of today — all of these are a deviation from the norm that needs a certain legal context in order to exist and to be used properly. It is not enough to say that PMCs are unethical and should be banned. Rather, an industry worth over $100 billion a year[97] should not remain unregulated. An adequate separation between legitimate and criminal initiatives must be established.

My unique analysis of British colonial activities illustrates the legal gaps in classification and organisation of military power. On one hand, it mirrors contemporary state behaviours in their attempts to bypass the law through outsourcing the military functions to a non-state organisation. On the other, it highlights the importance of codification of undefined military forces today. Breaking through the customary notions of 'public' and 'private' helps to reveal the private military sector as an inherent form of force used by states throughout history rather than a new phenomenon. While the institutionalisation of the national army created a strong rationale against the use of mercenaries and foreign legions, marking their normative decline and delegitimisation, colonial ambitions introduced European powers to a brand

[96] See Thompson, 37.

[97] B. Yeoman, 'Soldiers of Good Fortune' (2003) *Mother Jones* at <http://www.motherjones.com/politics/2003/05/soldiers-good-fortune>.

new pool of unclassified military resources. Neither mercenary nor national, these forces formed an integral part of colonial armies, highlighting the differentiation between public and private in a military context. as a legal and normative paradox, this is one historical example that demonstrates states' methods of removing responsibility in the pursuit of their sovereign needs.

There are without a doubt numerous hurdles to overcome on a national and international level to implement a viable regulatory structure. In recent years the UN General Assembly Working Group on the use of mercenaries has been following the development of the Policy and Operations Manual on the use of armed services from private security companies. Furthermore, the Working Group is engaging with the Department of Safety and Security in order to contribute to the development of a coherent, human rights-compliant policy framework for the procurement and use of armed private security companies by the United Nations organs and bodies.[98] Despite all efforts however, currently neither the UN Human Rights Council nor the General Assembly distinguishes between mercenaries, PMCs and PSCs, hindering international community's ability to formulate the norms.

While the diffusion of state control poses significant challenges to the regulation of PMCs, it also demonstrates the need for such regulation. Looking back through history, the only types of governance that achieved successful monopoly of public violence were those entirely powered by, and engrossed in, state militarism. Perhaps in our contemporary international state system, private forces would naturally find room to exist? In the political and legal context of declining state sovereignty and with the rise and active participation of non-state actors, private military companies are thriving and expanding their clientele from states to international corporations.

Finally, appropriate codification under international law, and increased state responsibility, would allow for effective regulation of the private security sector. This would leave only legitimate players in the market and draw a clear line, for both states and individuals, under the rules of employing mercenaries.

---

[98] A/HRC/24/45, para. 11, 4–5.

Court of Arbitration for Sport: The Effectiveness of CAS Awards and FIFA

Matteo Maciel[†]

This article examines the minute and fascinating relationship between the Court of Arbitration for Sport (CAS) and the international governing body for association football, FIFA. This paper will attempt to examine how effective the CAS has been. It will tease out whether subsequent complicate within FIFA occurs and why the judicial principles of the CAS provide a sobering voice within FIFA. Additionally, in examining the close relationship the CAS has with FIFA, it will become clear why FIFA is capable of extracting unanimous adherence to CAS findings. In essence, it creates an international regime in which compliance is a tacit criterion of participation. Examining FIFA through the lens of international political theory authorizes a fascinating perspective on the CAS and its relationship. It is the organization's structure and operation as an international regulator that contributes to CAS award adherence. To facilitate this journey, one must first understand the role FIFA plays in international sport, and the type of relationships it has with subsidiary members.

Keywords: FIFA, Court of Arbitration for Sport, international regime, effectiveness, law.

1. Introduction

Association football is one of the most popular sports in the world.[1] Its accessibility and popularity consistently attract billions of spectators every

---

[†] LLB Candidate, University of York Law School; B.A., University of Western Ontario.

year. Under the international regulating body, Fédération Internationale de Football Association (FIFA), football is a global business. In order to mediate an international sport, FIFA has created a regime in which to regulate its various (and varying) member organizations. More nations adhere to, and participate in, FIFA than the United Nations.[2] The governing body oversees some of the most expensive sport markets in the world. It was estimated that in 2004 the average worth of the twenty most valuable soccer clubs was 443 million U.S. dollars, with FIFA alone recording revenue in excess of 4.8 billion U.S. dollars.[3]

The global nature of football, its popularity, and the number of contracts and agreements made between organizational bodies means that business practices will inevitably come into dispute. These disputes cross international jurisdictions and create unique challenges for regulators. FIFA's role as a regulator is facilitated by an *ad hoc* relationship with the CAS. The increasingly active role of an international court serving to arbitrate football disputes raises the question of how 'effective' FIFA arbitration by the CAS has been in resolving disputes and obtaining compliance. This paper will uncover how the internationality of football operates, why an international body like FIFA is needed, and how FIFA's structure and place as an international regulator contributes to a high level of compliance to CAS awards.

2. Compliance

Compliance is what makes FIFA and the CAS extremely effective. The CAS adds vital jurisprudence principles to FIFA, but it is FIFA's ability to extract compliance from its members that is noteworthy. The power to wield compliance is extended to the CAS in its role as arbitrator. It is this relationship which is most intriguing. Compliance results from FIFA statutes holding legal force on its members. FIFA's regulations may be understood in as 'law-like'[4] because they are limited in their application beyond FIFA members. The CAS's position as an independent and impartial arbitrator fulfills judicial due process and in doing so allows arbitrational awards to influence FIFA's relationship with sporting Clubs as a private contract with resulting obligations, rights, and remedies. As a result, CAS's awards are

---

[1] Eric Dunning, *Sport Matters: Sociological Studies of Sport, Violence and Civilisation* (2nd edn, Routledge 1999) 80-106.

[2] FIFA, 'FIFA Statutes: Regulations Governing the Application of the Statutes Standing Orders Of The Congress' (Fédération Internationale de Football Association 2013).

[3] Ibid.

[4] Scott Shapiro, *Legality* (Harvard University Press 2011), 60, 163

institutionally binding, providing a unique example of a effective system of compliance.

The tenet of this argument is that the nature of FIFA's governance ought to be imagined in the international system as a hierarchal web. To help describe how the system works and the role of FIFA, the English football Association will be used as an example. Domestically, a governing body known as an Association regulates football. The entity oversees all levels of the game, including amateur and professional leagues, and is responsible for enforcing equality, fair play principles, and the laws of the game.[5] In the case of England, the body is known as 'the Football Association'(or simply, the FA). Association traditionally creates a hierarchal system of divisions. Again, for reference, the highest level of football in England is the 'Premier League' followed by 'Football League Championship' and so on.[6] This system facilitates a promotion and relegation scheme where performances resulting in success throughout the sporting season equates to promotion into the league above. By contrast, failures resulting in a match record worse than competing teams will translate to relegation to the league below. The threat of relegation creates a vicious incentive for competition as well as demand for investment into personnel. Successful teams, especially those in top-flight divisions generate large revenues. The potential for ever growing revenues has resulted in modern professional football being defined by talent hunting in order to create and maintain competitive teams.[7]

The hierarchy extends beyond the FA in order to provide more opportunities for global revenues. This results in international competitions, with access being awarded only as a result of seasonal success. '[T]o maintain the structure of the football pyramid, the leagues, as bodies representing the clubs, must be subordinate to the associations', who are members not only of FIFA, but also of 'continental governing bodies'.[8] This structure creates a complex web, cutting across dozens of legal jurisdictions. The relationship between associations and FIFA works both ways. The associations confer power to FIFA, but it is FIFA's recognition of those associations that make them legitimate.[9] Unlike American sports, football Clubs do not exercise revenue sharing. As a result, consistent success equates to substantial wealth—often used to sign athletes capable of bring further successes. In

---

[5] FIFA Statutes (n 2). See also The Football Association, 'The FA Handbook 2015-16' (The Football Association 2015).

[6] Ibid., 165.

[7] Ibid.

[8] *All about FIFA* (1st edn, Fédération Internationale de Football Association 2015) <http://www.fifa.com/mm/document/fifafacts/organisation/02/13/11/06/03072013allaboutfifa_neutral.pdf> accessed 30 March 2014.

[9] Bruno Simma, 'Court of Arbitration for Sport' in *The Court of Arbitration for Sport, 1984-2004* (1st edn, TMC Asser Press 2006), 22.

order to understand the effects of FIFA and ultimately the CAS, one must first understand the historical significance of player transfers and the vital role played by FIFA regulations.

3. History of Player Transfer and FIFA Regulations

The progression from associated amateur sport to professional was well underway by the late 1880's and 'the [Football] Association introduced a regulatory system that allowed it to oversee the transfer of professional players from one club to another'.[10] The 'retain and transfer' system became immensely popular. It set a fee that, if matched, allowed a Club access to contract negotiation with a given player. Until the Court of Justice of the European Union case *Union Royale Belge des Societes de Football Association (ASBL) v Bosman*[11], players were forced to remain on a team until a transfer fee was offered—even under circumstances where the wage contract had expired.[12] A transfer fee is like purchasing the rights to negotiate a contract with the player. The result was a market of buying and selling rights to negotiations. Teams were able to either purchase talent needed to win games or sell players for profit.

While the formation of regulated contracts was taking shape in England, football began to spread in popularity across Europe. By 1904, many other countries had established football associations, eight of whom founded FIFA in Paris during May of that year.[13] Over the course of the century, FIFA found itself as an international regulator for several reasons: (1) in attempts to seek bigger markets and greater success, teams began to transfer players between the top-flight leagues of Europe;[14] (2) the spread of football created a high demand of a unified regulatory body[15]; and (3) these same market forces brought a demand for international cooperation and competition by way of tournament.[16] The scale at which FIFA and the sport grew was substantial, and resulted in greater numbers of issues regarding transfers, inter-team and association disputes, and other regulatory matters.

---

[10] David McArdle, 'One Hundred Years of Servitude: Contractual Conflict In English Professional Football Before Bosman' [2000] Web Journal of Current Legal Issues <http://archive.today/9RfY#selection-411.468-411.617> accessed 31 March 2015.

[11] Case C-415/93 *Royale Belge des Societes de Football Association (ASBL) v Bosman* [1996] All E.R. (EC) 97, para 48.

[12] Ibid.

[13] Fédération Internationale de Football Association, 'A Success for the Entire Football Community' (2015) <http://www.fifa.com/aboutfifa/organisation/administration/news/newsid=2568019/index.html.> accessed 28 March 2015.

[14] Ibid.

[15] Ibid.

[16] Ibid.

When it comes to FIFA's structure and regulations, one may imagine a creation of 'law-like' rules that apply only to its members. The result is a description which is extremely similar to Stephen Krasner's international institutional regime.[17] In participating in the sport of football, recognizing and being recognized by FIFA; teams, associations, and leagues create a social contract where tacit and explicit consent authorizes the creation of regulation and subsequent enforcement.

According to Article 68 of the Swiss Zivilgestzbuch, FIFA operates as a non-profit organization applying private law unto voluntary actors.[18] In the world of sport, FIFA governs all actors, organizations, and events that pertain to football, its play, or operation.[19] In this way, the sport of football is FIFA's private property, "including copyrights which [...] may [be] exploited commercially'.[20] Due to the increasing international nature of the sport, a large part of FIFA's role involved imposing fair practices onto association football 'in the spirit of the game'.[21] This included efforts to uphold the integrity of football through mitigating unfair business practices, exterminating racism, regulating match officials, and punishing game-fixing. All of these efforts convey advantages for international institutions according to Robert Keohane and Lisa Martian in 'The Promise of Insitutionalist Theory'.[22] Keohane describes norms and principles as actions that buttress an international regime. FIFA's regulatory statutes serve as norms, and as a result, the statutes elicit obligatory compliance. To participate in the commercial elements of football, members must comply with the resulting norms. We will see that this comes from exclusionary reasons, which result in high levels of legal compliance and enables CAS awards high revere.

In enforcing an increasing level of decisions, FIFA's arbitrational system utilizes the International Olympic Committee's (IOC) CAS. FIFA statutes place CAS as an independent arbitrational body designed to handle 'disputes of a non-technical nature which no [subsidiary] body [wa]s competent to resolve'.[23] The CAS's role as an arbitrator is predominantly limited to player transfers and disputes arising from FIFA statute interpretation and enforcement.[24] CAS serves as an appeal for disputes and rulings made within the football system. By acting as an appeal court, CAS bridges the gap

---

[17] Stephen D. Krasner, 'Structural Causes And Regime Consequences: Regimes As Intervening Variables' (1982) 36 International Organization, 185-205.
[18] Simma, 22.
[19] FIFA Statutes, *supra.*
[20] Simma, 22.
[21] FIFA Statutes, *supra.*
[22] Robert O. Keohane and Lisa L. Martin, 'The Promise Of Institutionalist Theory' (1995) 20 International Security, 48-49.
[23] Simma, 24.
[24] Ibid.

between various legal jurisdictions and the law-like jurisdiction of FIFA. In doing so, the CAS is able to avoid contentious questions regarding on field decisions as per *Mendy v Association Internationale de Boxing Amateur*[25], and rather remains focused on the application of FIFA's private law norms to FIFA's members.[26] The intrinsic link between player, club, and governing body is assembled in a form not dissimilar to a federalist system where contractual obligations are vertically integrated while still holding horizontal duties. The English Court of Appeal confirmed the existence of relationship between athlete and governing body in *Modahl v British Athletic Federation Ltd (No. 2),*[27] and the resulting dicta delineated a complex contractual relationship that resembled a private norm system.

As mentioned above, transfers of players throughout FIFA subsidiaries is an expensive and comprehensive business practice. At the time of writing, the record transfer fee was 77 million pounds sterling paid between top league teams; the English-based Tottenham Hotspurs and Spanish Club Real Madrid. This fee was paid for the opportunity to negotiate a contract with one player, Welshmen Gareth Bale, who was subsequently paid £300,000 a week.[28] The current price listed in the release clause for Bale's teammate Cristiano Ronaldo is a staggering 750 million pounds.[29] FIFA statutes outline rules and restrictions pertaining to transfers that serve to solve issues regarding when offers may be made, the types of offers, how old players must be, the maximum number of teams they may play on a year, and, as seen above, conditions for automatically triggering a transfer. The nature of transfer contracts is such that the validity of the contract in law is traditionally not in dispute. *Lex loci solutionis* and *lex loci contractus* (as well as FIFA statutes on transfers) make most transfers legal under national law. Where the CAS frequently becomes involved is not in the domestic legality of the contract but rather when the validity of the contract regarding FIFA statutes is in contention.

4. THE LEGAL THEORY

The CAS, as an independent arbitrational body, has a unique role to fill within the context of the international sport community. The habitual rulings

---

[25] *Mendy v Association Internationale de Boxing Amateur* CAS 1996/H/OG Atlanta 1996/06
[26] Ibid.
[27] [2002] 1 W.L.R. 1192.
[28] Peter-Joseph Hegarty and Alex Duff, 'Gareth Bale Joins Real Madrid From Spurs On 6-Year Contract' *Bloomberg* (2013) <http://www.bloomberg.com/news/articles/2013-09-01/bale-to-join-real-madrid-tottenham-manager-villas-boas-says> accessed 30 March 2014.
[29] Simon Rice, 'Christian Ronaldo Release Clause Confirmed: Real Madrid Exit Could Be Triggered at 750M' *The Independent UK* (2015).

create an institutional norm that buttresses an institutional regime. 'Norms,' says Krasner, 'are standards of behavior defined in terms of rights and obligation'.[30] The resulting relationship between international sport regulators and the CAS is one that completes a holistic legal regime of procedures and norms that extracts compliance.[31] This compliance is so overt that it is not far off from a Lockeian conception of the social contract.[32] To fail to adhere to FIFA and the CAS is to undermine the institutional regime—violate norms—and consequently the social contract that exists between FIFA and its entities. The CAS case *Mendy*[33] established a vertical contract and hints at the fact that the obligations between FIFA and its members are binding. In regards to FIFA, CAS serves 'without the taint of influence from sporting organizations'.[34] CAS's relationship with FIFA generates what Joseph Raz would define as 'exclusionary reasons'.[35] Raz's *Theory of Practical Reason and Norms* teased out exclusionary reasons as negative second-order reasons.[36] An exclusionary reason occurs when circumstances force actors to disregard an action entirely. The disregard originates from a primary stimulant, which instead encourages the actor to exclude the possibility of acting a certain way based purely on the initial stimulant.[37] Raz's example of military orders as excluding the merit of moral reasons in his book is of particular noteworthiness, it sheds light on how FIFA's control over professional football excludes reasons to violate regulation.[38] Here we may integrate Keohane's description of Insitutionalist regimes once again, Keohane describes institutions as facilitating cooperation via norms. Below we will see why this is the case.

---

[30] Krasner, *supra.*
[31] Ibid.
[32] John Locke and C.B. Macpherson, *Second Treatise Of Government* (1st edn, Hackett Publishing Co, Inc 1980).
[33] *Mendy, supra.*
[34]Richard McLaren, 'Twenty-Five Years Of The Court Of Arbitration For Sport: A Look In The Rear-View Mirror' (2010) 20 Marquette Sports Law Review <http://scholarship.law.marquette.edu/cgi/viewcontent.cgi?article=1482&context=sportslaw> accessed 29 March 2014, 305-33. <http://scholarship.law.marquette.edu/cgi/viewcontent.cgi?article=1482&context=sportslaw. There is an example, found in *Raguz v. Sullivan*, which exemplifies that even though CAS appeals may occur within other nations, sometimes entirely within one nation, the institution in Lausanne remains the appropriate site to resolve disputes, even if the first instance of CAS is in Australia. The Swiss Federal Tribunal has found the CAS to be consistently independent and impartial despite arbitrating between members and the IOC. This factor will become a key element in deciding whether CAS is effective in international arbitration.
[35] Shapiro, 30-53.
[36] Ibid.
[37] Joseph Raz, *Practical Reason And Norms* (Princeton University Press 1990), 38.
[38] Ibid.

5. CASE LAW

There are three international law cases that display why FIFA's control over members is interesting when compared to the traditional state-based international system. The International Court of Justice decision in *Nicaragua v. United States*[39] establishes the recognition of state sovereignty within the international system. In the English Court of Appeal case of *R v Disciplinary Committee of the Jockey Club,*[40] Sir Thomas Bingham M.R. delineates the limits of England and Wales courts into consensual contracts formed with the governing bodies found in sports. In establishing that the relationship formed a private contract, Lord Diplock, in *Council of Civil Service Unions v Minister for the Civil Service,* said that if the power originated from contract and a private arbitrator was assigned, there was no room for judicial review.[41] *Disciplinary Committee of the Jockey Club* established that private contracts could create private rights and obligations. Resulting disputes regarding these private rights and obligations ought to be determined via private arbitrators.[42] The level of involvement through Judicial Review varies across the European Union, generally there is the acknowledgement of a link between FIFA and its members. The CAS has a crucial role in the contractual framework created to support FIFA, its role as an independent judicial arbitrator solicits (1) recognition of an international mechanism to solve disputes; and (2) helps centralize universal and consistent application of sport specific precedent across a wide range of international jurisdictions.[43] The private contract between FIFA and its members authorizes the CAS 'to facilitate the settlement of disputes of a private nature arising out of the practice or development of sport'.[44] The system generates 'a unique example of a private international legal regime that has almost entirely displaced domestic adjudication of certain types of disputes'.[45] The result is an international regime of norms which have been allowed to develop independent regulatory powers[46]

What is of particular interest is the effectiveness of compliance amongst the international systems. Below, I will explore the theoretical grounds for

---

[39] Case Concerning *Military and Paramilitary Activities in and against Nicaragua (Nicaragua v. United States of America)* Jurisdiction and Admissibility, Judgment [1986] ICJ Rep 392.
[40] [1993] 1 W.L.R. 909.
[41] Ibid.
[42] Ibid, 939 C.
[43] Ibid.
[44] Simma, 22.
[45] Annie Bersagel, 'Is there a Stare Decisis Doctrine in the Court of Arbitration for Sport? An Analysis of Published Awards for Anti-Doping Disputes in Track and Field' [2012] 2 Pepp. Disp. Resol. L.J. 189.
[46] Lord Denning MR in *Enderby Town Football Club v Football Association* [1971] Ch 591, para 602.

why FIFA can extract compliance while organizations like the United Nations cannot. This article will show that such compliance derives from a Krasner-like 'international regime theory'. The CAS's work with FIFA must first establish the case for effectiveness. For this to be true, the CAS's findings must be shown to be: (1) consistently enforced, and (2) not grossly negligent of principles of the rule of law.

In the Standard Statutes, FIFA, 'its members, players, Officials and match and player's agents will not take any dispute to Ordinary Courts unless specifically provided for in the Statutes and FIFA regulations'.[47] The outlining of these limits is consistent with *Disciplinary Committee of the Jockey Club* referenced above. The failure to comply with 'any final decision passed by a FIFA body or CAS.[48] will result in disciplinary actions, which may include warnings, transfer bans, relegation to lower divisions, and even expulsion.[49] Two cases in particular are noteworthy for displaying the enforcement of FIFA and the CAS. *Tareq Eltaib v. Club Gaziantepspor*[50] establishes 'just cause' as grounds for termination of an employment contract. It is an award useful to this paper in two ways. First, it establishes that FIFA regulations 'caseharden globally the system of contractual relations and its stability in football'.[51] Second, the case ought to be used as an example of the level of compliance the CAS exerts. In the *Tareq* case, the CAS decided that the termination in question was not justified and ordered the Player back to the Club before outlining the compensation to be paid from the Player to the Club for the violation. In doing so, *Tareq* exhibits the existence of a private social contract formed through a chain of contractual obligations and rights, all of which are underpinned through, at least in England and Wales, by the crucial notion of contractual consent. In *Luis Suarez, FC Barcelona & AUF v. FIFA*[52] the CAS conveyed independence and impartiality when scrutinizing FIFA's application of disciplinary regulations, ultimately finding the sanctions placed onto the Player were disproportionate.[53]The *Suarez* case demonstrates the impartiality Richard McLarean discusses when he references the Swiss Federal Tribunal case *G v Fédération Equestre Internationale and Court of Arbitration for Sport*[54] which resulted in substantial reform to the CAS, allowing it to be impartial even in scenarios arbitrating where the IOC was a party.

---

[47] FIFA Statutes, s66(1).
[48] Ibid., s67(2).
[49] Ibid., s64.
[50] *Tareq Eltaib v. Club Gaziantepspor* [2006] CAS 2006/A/1100 2006, paras 1-15.
[51] Ibid., para 22.
[52] *Luis Suarez, FC Barcelona & AUF v. FIFA* [2014] CAS 2014/A/3665 2014, para 78l; see also cases 3666 & 3667, 2014.
[53] Ibid.
[54] CAS, Arrêt Du Tribunal Fédéral Suisse, 1st Civil Division, 15 March 1993.

In *FC Schalke, FC Barcelona, & SV Werder Bremen v. Fédération Internationale de Football Association (FIFA)*[55], CAS awarded in favour of the clubs and concluded that FIFA was to bear the brunt and consequences of poorly worded regulations, including paying certain fees. There are strong similarities between the case and the examples shown by Ran Hirschl regarding the spread of constitutionalism and judicialization in domestic legal systems. CAS decisions remove FIFA from the ultimate decision-making process and judicialize the decision-making processes.

CAS compliance is extremely high. In the last forty FIFA cases heard by the CAS not one resulted in a member failing to comply. In the CAS award *Suarez & others*[56], FIFA was found to be at fault and was forced to make concessions regarding its own prior actions. I could not locate any examples of non-compliance to FIFA related CAS awards in the research conducted. The frequency of cases heard by the CAS regarding FIFA is also an important factor, especially noting the high level of compliance observed within the system. Since 2000, nearly 200 FIFA related cases have been appealed to CAS.[57] *FC Politehnica Timisoara SA v. FIFA & Romanian Football Federation* acknowledges CAS's *Lex Sportiva,* when 'FIFA informs a Club that the 'case was closed…the decision is [still] susceptible to an appeal to CAS'.[58] The case highlights that FIFA's decisions are binding, but are subject to appeal to CAS. It creates a framework for preexisting *ratio decidendi* that CAS awards are enforceable even onto FIFA. The decisions establish the CAS as an independent, impartial and fair arbitrator.

6. Independence and Impartiality

As mentioned above, there is the question of impartiality or lack thereof. The lack of separation between judge and litigant is a principle, according to Scott Shapiro, that undermines the central premise of judicial decisions.[59] As in domestic legal systems, arbitration relies on independent adjudication to its decisions to be seen as legitimate. In being initially set up by the IOC as an arbitrational entity, the CAS's financial structure is also an important factor. Demarcating from the former IOC funding scheme, arbitration fees are paid

[55] *FC Schalke, FC Barcelona, & SV Werder Bremen v. Fédération Internationale de Football Association (FIFA)* [2008] CAS 2008/A/1622, 1623, 1624, para 1-3, 58-60.
[56] *Suarez,* para 77.
[57] McLaren, 305–333.
[58] *FC Politehnica Timisoara SA v. FIFA & Romanian Football Federation (RFF) & Politehnica Stintia 1921 Timisoara Invest SA* [2007] CAS 2007/A/1355.
[59] Shapiro, 73.

by the parties involved in the arbitration.[60] This decouples financial influences that could play a factor in sport arbitration.

In a landmark Swiss Federal Tribunal (SFT) case, the court made it clear that:

> the CAS is sufficiently independent *vis-a-vis* the IOC, as well as all other parties that call upon its services, for its decisions in cases […] to be considered true awards, equivalent to the judgments of State courts.[61]

Not long after, the SFT concluded that FIFA's ability to fine members for a failure to comply with CAS was not an infringement on the state monopoly to enforce monetary judgments and was justified.[62]

An entirely internal appeals procedure would not only place the impartiality of the decisions in jeopardy, but it could also undermine the value of an appeal entirely. In *Luis Suarez v FIFA*, an appeal to the FIFA disciplinary appeals board resulted in no change. When the case reached the CAS, the disciplinary ruling was overturned.[63] This is significant because it shows that appeals to the CAS have altered traditional norms of FIFA being the highest level of arbitration and resulted in a more equitable (if not a judicial) process of interpreting FIFA statutes. 'The CAS adds a layer of scrutiny to internal hearings, creating a fairer, more transparent procedure'.[64] The outcome is not only a more effective arbitration entity, but also a more legitimate one.

7. Regular and Consistent?

Looking at the effectiveness of the CAS affords the opportunity to test whether compliance within the FIFA system is regular and consistent. This paper argues that it is. CAS awards are rarely violated due to the threat of regulators imposing sanctions for violations.[65] Even without FIFA statutes,

---

[60] Abbas Ravjani, 'The Court Of Arbitration For Sport: A Subtle Form Of International Delegation' (2009) 2 Journal of International Media & Entertainment Law <http://go.galegroup.com/ps/i.do?id=GALE|A198547944&v=2.1&u=lond95336&it=r&p=AONE&sw=w&authCount=1> accessed 29 March 2014.

[61] Ibid.

[62] Roy Levi. "Swiss Federal Tribunal Overrules CAS Award in a Landmark Decision: *FIFA vs Matuzalem*." The International Sports Law Journal 36. <http://www.probst-law.ch/bilder/The-International-Sports-Law-Journal-2012.pdf>.

[63] *Suarez,* para 78.

[64] Ibid.

[65] Rui Botica Santos, Alexandre Mestre and Francisco Raposo de Magalhães, *Sports Law In Portugal* (Kluwer Law International 2011). Part 1, chapter 1.F, para 281.

CAS awards host substantial teeth in regards to their ability to impose compliance. In addition to financial sanctions, the awards are in line with the New York Convention on the Recognition and Enforcement of Foreign Arbitral Awards (1958),[66] and thus CAS decisions have international enforcement through national legal frameworks across the globe.[67] The international agreement sustains traditional rules of law found in the Jesse Lewis Claim, *United States v. Great Britain* (1921), that leaves the application and interpretation of the law to the discretion of tribunals. In other words, the CAS has the ability to force compliance through domestic rule of law systems by virtue of the 1958 Convention.

There are examples of teams attempting to exploit the system, but no explicit examples of failures to comply with CAS. In the summer transfer window of 2014, Barcelona FC received severe sanctions for breaching regulations in signing players under the age of 18. In appeal, Barcelona FC used the opportunity to delay the transfer ban and acquire players. For using the appeal delay to acquire more players, CAS fined the Club an additional €300,000, a relatively small amount compared to the money spent throughout the window, but still a substantial punishment.[68]

The high level of compliance exists as the central tenant to arguing the CAS's effectiveness, especially in the international system. In addition to compliance, CAS is timely with an arbitration time limit of four months.[69] The role of CAS creates an independent appeal system fulfilling vital elements of jurisprudence.[70] CAS has consistently proven its impartiality and diligence, within and beyond FIFA—another concept deemed crucial to law-like systems. Lastly, the formation of private contract between FIFA and its members helps elicit the binding nature of CAS awards. These three elements make CAS an effective arbitrational entity.

The high level of compliance ought also to be explained by imagining the regulations as institutional norms and practices, buttressing FIFA as an international regime supporting a private social contract. Krasner's description of international bodies describes how sanctions come to play a crucial role in the international regime.[71] Failure to comply with this contract has legitimate and enforceable sanctions but only within the system itself. The most severe

---

[66] Ibid.

[67] Jesse Lewis Claim, *United States v. Great Britain* (1921).

[68] Simon Jones, 'Barcelona Blast CAS Ruling As Club's Appeal Against 2015 Signings Ban Is Rejected' *Daily Mail Online* (2014) <http://www.dailymail.co.uk/sport/football/article-2891100/Barcelona-s-appeal-against-ban-new-signings-2015-rejected-FIFA-decision-upheld-Court-Arbitration-Sport.html> accessed 29 March 2015.

[69] Ravjani, 254.

[70] Shapiro, 163. Shapiro states that separation between judges and members of the dispute is important to maintain a fair and legitimate system.

[71] Krasner, 185–205.

of these sanctions is a suspension of participation in the sport. The acknowledgment and delineation of this chain of contracts is the final stage in explaining why the CAS is effective and how theoretical compliance (through this contract) has translated into legitimate compliance. Identifying which theorist is best suited in application to FIFA is a substantial question, and one that could be the topic of an entire article on its own. For this paper, simply identifying that FIFA is an institutional regime will be sufficient.

FIFA's international institutional regime is, in theory, utilitarian, and its origins convey strong shades of John Rawls' progression out of the state of nature and into a system which is mutually beneficial for all members.[72] Rawls' veil of ignorance claims that if all members of an agreement were to not know their own strengths or the strengths of others, members would be inclined to create a community with fair policies that do not marginalize the least benefited. Participating in an international regime for the benefits it provides is a core concept of liberal international theory. Outside the context of sovereignty, the international regime posits as a possible explanation. Sovereignty impedes a central regulator in the international system, whereas FIFA is founded upon regime norms, principles, and practices. Krasner examples Susan Strange to conceive regimes as a structural orientation in line with 'rational self-seeking actors…They function in a system or environment that is defined by their own interests, power, and integration.'[73] In other words, the international social contract is a convincing hypothesis for helping explain why the CAS extracts conformity through the FIFA system. In eliciting consent, the governing body draws upon, not only its own power, but also the power of judicial jurisdictions. By conceiving the relationship between governing body and members, *R v Disciplinary Committee of the Jockey Club* entrenches the notion that private regimes are formed upon contractual agreements. Courts, at least those of England and Wales, are limited in their capacity to go beyond the contracts and provide remedy under specific performance.[74] The private obligations, conveyed as a contract, helps explain why CAS awards pertaining to FIFA are consistently adhered to. Sovereign states, in contrast, are conveyed as consistently failing to conform with the international system.

Corruption within FIFA is a major concern that cannot be ignored in any academic paper hoping to discuss the hierarchal structure of the organization and its resulting effectiveness. Substantial evidence implicates the

---

[72] See John Rawls, *A Theory of Justice* (Harvard University Press.1999) 118. See also Byers, Terri, Trevor Slack, and Milena Parent. *Key Concepts in Sport Management* (Los Angeles: SAGE, 2012), 65.

[73] Krasner, 191.

[74] Ewan McKendrick, *Contract Law: Texts, Cases, And Materials* (6th edn, Oxford University Press 2014).

organization in match-fixing and other illegal activities.[75] Despite the recent indictments, little academic research has been done on the topic.[76] Corruption indubitably undermines efforts at fair play and manufactures unfair advantages, these actions serve to weaken the international regime formed by FIFA with its members.[77] Two points must be made in regard to corruption for the sake of having addressed it in this paper. First, corruption does not serve to undermine the level of compliance that CAS awards elicit. The CAS, as an independent and impartial arbitrator, creates an inclination to seek out the CAS, to actively utilize it and to comply with its decisions.[78] In fact, the impartial nature of the CAS may serve to help legitimize FIFA amid charges that create irreconcilable damages to the reputation of the sport and its governing body. The CAS seeks not to reverse match calls made by officials, a policy which falls in line with Lord Denning's *orbiter* in *Enderby Town Football Club v Football Association*[79] which exempts match activities from judicial scrutiny so long as due diligence occurred.[80] While this does not speak to the issues pertaining to FIFA corruption or the effects on the private contract, its discussion here aims to mitigate any arguments that compliance to CAS awards are as a result of corruption within the system. Second, while corruption undermines the private social contract between FIFA and its members, the aim of this article is to examine the effectiveness of CAS awards in regard to FIFA, and does not explore corruptions consequences on that effectiveness. To determine effectiveness, the paper outlined three elements of due process. When compared to other international arbitrational bodies, the relationship between FIFA and CAS is highly efficient while still maintaining principles reflective of key standards of justice. That is to say, while FIFA corruption may undermine fair play principles of the game and the reputation of the sport, there is no evidence to suggest that it undermines the effectiveness of CAS appeals originating from FIFA.[81]

---

[75] Owen Gibson and Damien Gayle, FIFI Officials Arrested on Corruption Charges as World Cup Inquiry Launched' *The Guardian UK* (2015) <http://www.theguardian.com/football/2015/may/27/several-top-fifa-officials-arrested> accessed 29 October 2015.

[76] Krasner, 191.

[77] Ibid.

[78] McLaren, 306.

[79] [1971] Ch 591.

[80] *Suarez, supra*; Mendy, *supra.*

[81] Michaël Mrkonjic, 'Sports Organizations, Autonomy and Good Governance' (Play the Game/ Danish Institute for Sport Studies 2013) <http://dspace.mah.se/dspace/bitstream/handle/2043/17866/AGGIS_Final_report.pdf?sequence=2&isAllowed=y#page=133> accessed 29 March 2015.

8. CONCLUSION

FIFA's regulatory regime is a unique anomaly in an international system often portrayed as inconsistent. Even liberal theorists must concede that international compliance and cooperation are rarely seen on the scale or consistency that may be observed through FIFA compliance with the CAS. This compliance is not by coincidence. This paper has outlined several contributing reasons that have helped formulate a private law regime cultivating a high level of compliance to the CAS. As a result of fulfilling key tenets of judicial practice, and in being supported by domestic case law, the CAS is sought after, actively utilized, and consistently adhered to. It forms an environment, as a result of FIFA principles, in which CAS awards hold substantial clout in the international football community and as a result are complied with. CAS's fulfilling principles of judicial practice, the right to impartial appeals, an independent mediator, and a timely trial, are built upon the FIFA culture designed to nurture universal compliance with the private regime. FIFA's use of the CAS as a mediator entrenches core values of legal procedure and encases precedent for future use. In tandem with FIFA, CAS mediation of FIFA regulations portrays a unique example of a highly effective international regime supported not only by international norms, but also by domestic judicial systems.

References

All About FIFA (1st edn, Federacion Internationale de Football Association 2015) <http://www.fifa.com/mm/document/fifafacts/organisation/02/13/11/06/03 072013allaboutfifa_neutral.pdf> accessed 30 March 2014.

Bersagel, A., 'Is There a Stare Decisis Doctrine in The Court of Arbitration for Sport? An Analysis of Published Awards for Anti-Doping Disputes in Track and Field' (2012) 12 Pepperdine Dispute Resolution Law Journal <http://digitalcommons.pepperdine.edu/cgi/viewcontent.cgi?article=1215 &context=drlj> accessed 31 March 2015.

Byers, T., T. Slack and M. Parent, *Key Concepts in Sport Management* (SAGE, 2012).

Conter, David, "Philosophy of Law". Lecture, from Huron University College at Western, London, November 5, 2014.

Danish Institute for Sport Studies, 'Sports Organizations, Autonomy and Good Governance' (Play the Game/ Danish Institute for Sport Studies 2013) <http://dspace.mah.se/dspace/bitstream/handle/2043/17866/AGGIS_Final _report.pdf?sequence=2&isAllowed=y#page=133> accessed 29 March 2015.

Dunning, E., Sport Matters: *Sociological Studies of Sport, Violence and Civilisation* (2nd edn, Routledge, 1999).

Federation Internationale de Football Association, 'A Success For The Entire Football Community' (2015) <http://www.fifa.com/aboutfifa/organisation/administration/news/newsid= 2568019/index.html.> accessed 28 March 2015.

FIFA, 'FIFA Statutes: Regulations Governing the Application of the Statutes Standing Orders of the Congress' (Federation Internationale de Football Association 2013).

Gibson, O. and D. Gayle, 'FIFA Officials Arrested on Corruption Charges As World Cup Inquiry Launched' *The Guardian UK* (2015) .<http://www.theguardian.com/football/2015/may/27/several-top-fifa-officials-arrested> accessed 29 October 2015.

Gilson, E., 'Exploring The Court of Arbitration for Sport' (2006) 98 Law Library Journal 98.

Hegarty, P. and A. Duff, 'Gareth Bale Joins Real Madrid from Spurts On 6-Year Contract' *Bloomberg* (2013) <http://www.bloomberg.com/news/articles/2013-09-01/bale-to-join-real-madrid-tottenham-manager-villas-boas-says> accessed 30 March 2014.

Jennings, A., 'Investigating Corruption in Corporate Sport: The IOC and FIFA' (2011) 46 International Review for the Sociology of Sport

<http://journals1.scholarsportal.info/pdf/10126902/v46i0004/387_icicstiaf.xml.> accessed 31 March 2015.

Jones, S., 'Barcelona Blast CAS Ruling As Club's Appeal Against 2015 Signings Ban Is Rejected' *Daily Mail Online* (2014) <http://www.dailymail.co.uk/sport/football/article-2891100/Barcelona-s-appeal-against-ban-new-signings-2015-rejected-FIFA-decision-upheld-Court-Arbitration-Sport.html> accessed 29 March 2015.

Keohane, R. and L. Martin, 'The Promise of Institutionalist Theory' (1995) 20 International Security.

Krasner, S., 'Structural Causes and Regime Consequences: Regimes As Intervening Variables' (1982) 36 International Organization.

Levi, R., 'Swiss Federal Tribunal Overrules CAS Award in Landmark Decision: *FIFA Vs Matuzalem*' [2012] The International Sports Law Journal.

Locke, J. and C. Macpherson, *Second Treatise of Government* (1st edn, Hackett Publishing Co, Inc., 1980).

McArdle, D., 'One Hundred Years of Servitude: Contractual Conflict in English Professional Football Before Bosman' [2000] Web Journal of Current Legal Issues <http://archive.today/9RfY#selection-411.468-411.617> accessed 31 March 2015.

McKendrick, E., *Contract Law: Texts, Cases, And Materials* (6th edn, Oxford University Press, 2014).

McLaren, R., 'Twenty-Five Years of the Court of Arbitration for Sport: A Look In The Rear-View Mirror' (2010) 20 Marquette Sports Law Review <http://scholarship.law.marquette.edu/cgi/viewcontent.cgi?article=1482&context=sportslaw> accessed 29 March 2014.

Mitten, M., 'The Court of Arbitration for Sport and Its Global Jurisprudence: International Legal Pluralism In A World Without National Boundaries' (2014) 30 Ohio State Journal on Dispute Resolution.

Morris, P., S. Morrow and P. Spink, 'EC Law and Professional Football: Bosman and Its Implications' (1996) 59 The Modern Law Review <http://onlinelibrary.wiley.com/doi/10.1111/j.1468-2230.1996.tb02701.x/abstract;jsessionid=D0A8A0635624F0A1E64084B26CB51754.f03t01.> accessed 31 March 2015.

Nafziger, J., *Transnational Law of Sports*.

Ravjani, A., 'The Court of Arbitration for Sport: A Subtle Form of International Delegation' (2009) 2 Journal of International Media & Entertainment Law <http://go.galegroup.com/ps/i.do?id=GALE|A198547944&v=2.1&u=lond95336&it=r&p=AONE&sw=w&authCount=1> accessed 29 March 2014

Rawls, J., *A Theory of Justice* (Harvard University Press 1999).

Raz, J., Practical Reason and Norms (Princeton University Press, 1990).

Rice, S., 'Christian Ronaldo Release Clause Confirmed: Real Madrid Exit Could Be Triggered at 750M' *The Independent* (2015).

Santos, R., A. Mestre and F. Magalhães, *Sports Law in Portugal* (Kluwer Law International, 2011).

Shapiro S, *Legality* (Harvard University Press, 2011).

Simma B, 'Court of Arbitration for Sport', The Court of Arbitration for Sport, 1984-2004 (1st edn, TMC Asser Press, 2006).

The Football Association, 'The FA Handbook 2015-16' (The Football Association 2015).

VerSteeg R, Sports Law (Vandeplas Pub, 2007).

VerSteeg R, *The Essentials of Greek and Roman Law* (Carolina Academic Press, 2010).

Case Concerning Military and Paramilitary Activities in and against Nicaragua (*Nicaragua v United States of America*) [1986] International Court of Justice, Rep 392 (International Court of Justice).

A Critical Analysis of the Commonly Recommended Reforms of Investor-State Dispute Settlement (ISDS)

Himaloya Saha[†]

Traditionally, investment disputes between foreign investors and host countries were resolved in the local courts of the host countries.[1] *However, developed countries tried to protect their foreign investors from discrimination and weak legal systems of developing countries and therefore resorted to international arbitration. The capacity of foreign investors to choose international arbitration as a dispute settlement mechanism gave rise to new problems.*[2] *The paper first examines the current investor-state dispute settlement regime under the International Convention on the Settlement of Investment Disputes (ICSID Convention) and United Nations Commission on International Trade law (UNCITRAL). It then identifies and analyzes the various criticisms of the current system. The next section of the paper aims at recognizing and evaluating the commonly proposed recommendations with a special focus on the ones by United Nations Convention on Trade and Development (UNCTAD). Lastly it is argued that the current challenges of the investor-state dispute settlement can only be improved by undertaking responsibilities of drafting exhaustive treaty provisions by the state parties and maintaining transparency and accountability by the arbitration forums.*

---

† LLM Candidate, University of Warwick School of Law.

1 Chen Huiping, 'The Investor-State Dispute Settlement Mechanism: Where To Go In The 21St Century?' (2008) 9 The Journal of World Investment & Trade, 467, 467.

2 Rodrigo Polanco Lazo, 'International Arbitration in Times of Change: Fairness and Transparency in Investor-State Disputes' (2010) 104 American Society of International Law, 591, 591.

Keywords: Investor State Dispute Settlement, International Arbitration, Foreign Investment

1. INTRODUCTION

Investor-State Dispute settlement (ISDS) clauses are a very common feature in International Investment Agreements (IIA) and Bilateral Investment Treaties (BIT).[3] The earliest BIT's like the German-Pakistan treaty signed in 1959 provides that disputes are to be settled by arbitration only when the parties disagree on the solution given by the by the International Court of Justice (ICJ) implementing the "spirit of friendship".[4] By the early 1990s there were widespread arbitration clauses in BIT's allowing the investors to bring claims against host state directly, thus starting the trend of ISDS mechanisms.[5] A study conducted by Organization for Economic Co-operation and Development (OECD)[6] in 2012 concludes that 93 per cent of the treaties now contain language on ISDS mechanism.[7] UNCTAD[8]'s most recent April 2014 review of ISDS development states that by the end of 2013, 98 states had responded to a total of 568 treaty-based claims since ISDS's inception.[9] This sudden increased number of cases have put the ISDS mechanism under scrutiny and is being criticized as being too investor-friendly.[10] As a result, countries like Bolivia, Ecuador and more recently Venezuela have already

---

[3] Ling Ling He, Razeen Sapideen, ' Investor-State Arbitration under Bilateral Trade and Investment Agreements: Finding Rhythm in Inconsistent Drumbeats' [2013] 47 Journal of World Trade, 215, 215.

[4] Dr. Christian Tietje, 'The Impact of Investor-State-Dispute Settlement (ISDS) in the Transatlantic Trade and Investment Partnership'(Study prepared for Minister for Foreign Trade and Development Cooperation, Ministry of Foreign Affairs, the Netherlands, MINBUZA-2014.78850, 24 June 2014) 7, 20.

[5] Ibid 22.

[6] 'About OECD '< http://www.oecd.org/about/ > accessed 8 December 2014.

[7] Joachim Paul, Kekeletso Mashigo, Alexis Nohan, 'Dispute Settlement Provisions in International Investment Agreements: A Large Sample Survey', (2012) OECD Working Papers on International Investment, 2012/02, OECD Publishing, 7, 8 < http://dx.doi.org/10.1787/5k8xb71nf628-en > accessed on 9 December 2014.

[8] United Nations Conference on Trade and Development < http://unctad.org/en/Pages/AboutUs.aspx >Accessed on 8 December 2014.

[9] UNCTAD, 'Recent Developments in Investor-State Dispute Settlement (ISDS)' (IIA Issues Note, No. 1, April 2014), 1.

[10] August Reinisch, 'The Scope of Investor-State Dispute Settlement in International Investment Agreements' (2013) 21 Asia Pacific Law Review 3, 4.

withdrawn from the International Centre for the Settlement of Investment Disputes, and terminated some of their BITs.[11] Australia in 2011 and India in 2012 also removed ISDS clauses in their future BIT's and Free Trade Agreements (FTA).[12] In response to this outcry, various recommendations have been suggested to mend the loopholes of the mechanism. This paper analyzes how effective the proposed recommendations are going to be. It is argued that the recommendations of the procedure will only have an impact when the treaties are precisely drafted giving little scope for interpretation to the arbitrators.

2. SALIENT FEATURES OF THE ISDS MECHANISM

The ISDS is a procedural mechanism that protects the foreign investors against any policy implemented by the host government that adversely affect their expected standard of treatment or cause economic harm under the investment agreement.[13] Under this mechanism, the investors can sue the host country government for compensation in the aforementioned cases in an international third-party arbitration tribunal.[14] The mechanism was designed to depoliticize investment disputes [15] and provide 'final and enforceable decisions through a swift, cheap, and flexible process, over which disputing parties would have considerable control'.[16]

Foreign investors as a part of their treaty could choose ISDS mechanisms like the ICSID Convention[17], ICSID's Additional Facility Rules[18] or the

---

[11] He and Sapideen (n3) 215-216.

[12] Ibid., 217.

[13] Daniel Ikenson, 'A Compromise to Advance the Trade Agenda: Purge Negotiations of Investor-State Dispute Settlement' (Cato Institute, 2014) Para 14 < http://www.cato.org/publications/free-trade-bulletin/compromise-advance-trade-agenda-purge-negotiations-investor-state > accessed 9 December 2014.

[14] Steffen Hinderlang,' Study on Investor-State Dispute Settlement (ISDS) and Alternatives of Dispute Resolution in International Investment Law (2014) Study for European Parliament's Committee on International Trade 2/2014,39 <http://papers.ssrn.com/sol3/papers.cfm?abstract_id=2525063> accessed 10 December 2014.

[15] Ibid.

[16] UNCTAD,'Reform of Investor State Dispute Settlements: In search of a Roadmap'(IIA Issues Note, No. 2, June2013), 2.

[17] The International Centre for Settlement of Investment Disputes (ICSID) is established by the Convention on the Settlement of Investment Disputes between States and Nationals of Other States (The ICSID Convention) in 1966 which provides facilities for conciliation and arbitration of investment disputes.< https://icsid.worldbank.org/ICSID/FrontServlet?requestType=CasesRH&actionVal=ShowHome&pageName=AboutICSID_Home > accessed on 10 December 2014.

[18] Ibid.

UNCITRAL Arbitration Rules[19] in order to bring a claim.[20] The ICSID Convention was applicable where both the respondent state and the claimant investor's home state have ratified the Convention and where only one of the above parties ratified the convention, ICSID's Additional Facility Rules were applied.[21] The UNICITRAL Arbitration rules alternatively apply when the parties have agreed to be bound by them.[22] The former requires exhaustion of domestic remedies and the consent of the parties in order to initiate a claim[23] whereas the latter requires a notice to be served to the other party.[24] Under both regimes there is provision for sole arbitrator or uneven number of arbitrators as agreed by the parties.[25] Any decision given by the respective tribunals are binding on both the parties.[26]

The ISDS was initiated as an instrument to enforce the rule of law by protecting international investors against arbitrary behaviour of host states and to guarantee them due process.[27] This system also ensures that the investors get fair and non-discriminatory treatment, compensation against expropriation which in turn encourages them to invest in a country ensuring the economic development of that country.[28] In addition, ISDS mechanism offers arbitrators, who are experts and highly qualified in the matter of the disputes, which domestic Courts can never accommodate. [29] This system provides confidentiality which might be highly desirable in order to avoid risks of revealing commercially sensitive information to contestants and also ensures

---

[19] United Nations commission on International Trade law (UNCITRAL) adopted the original UNCITRAL Arbitration Rules in 1976 and have been used for the settlement of a broad range of disputes, including disputes between private commercial parties where no arbitral institution is involved, investor-State disputes, State-to-State disputes and commercial disputes administered by arbitral institutions (The UNICITRAL Arbitration Rules). < http://www.uncitral.org/uncitral/en/uncitral_texts/arbitration/2010Arbitration_rules.html > accessed on 10 December 2014.

[20] Andrew P. Tuck, 'Investor-State Arbitration Revised: A Critical Analysis of the Revision and Proposed Reforms to the ICSID and UNCITRAL Arbitration Rules' [2007] Law and Business Review of the Americas 885, 885.

[21] The ICSID Convention, Article 25(1).

[22] The UNICITRAL Arbitration Rules, Article 1.

[23] The ICSID Convention, Article 26.

[24] The UNICITRAL Arbitration Rules, Article 3.

[25] The UNICITRAL Arbitration Rules, Article 8 and The ICSID Convention, Article 37.

[26] The UNICITRAL Arbitration Rules, Article 33 and The ICSID Convention, Article 53.

[27] Hinderlang (n14)40.

[28] www.uscib.org, 'Investor-State Dispute Settlement' (2014) < http://www.uscib.org/docs/2011_05_05_investor_to_state_brief.PDF > accessed 11 December 2014.

[29] Ibid.

transparency as information regarding the procedure is disclosed if both parties warrants it.[30]

3. CRITICISMS OF ISDS

The ISDS mechanism has been severely criticized. As Dr. Hinderlang notes, 'Critique of ISDS is as old as the system itself'.[31] The system has been deemed to be so futile that even the countries that had resorted to the mechanism as investment protection backed out.[32] The system has been severely criticized by the members of civil society,[33] experts,[34] international organizations[35] and the host countries[36]. The most significant criticisms of the ISDs are discussed below.

3.1. Superior Rights to Foreign Investors

National treatment is one of the basic structures of an investment treaty. It affirms that the foreign investors are to be treated in the same manner as the national investors and thereby be protected from discrimination.[37] ISDS

---

[30] James Politi, 'Does ISDS Strengthen or Weaken the Rule of Law? The Investor-State Dispute Settlement Mechanism: An Examination of Benefits and Costs' (CATO Institute 2014) < http://www.cato.org/events/investor-state-dispute-settlement-mechanism-examination-benefits-costs > accessed 11 December 2014.

[31] Hinderlang, 56.

[32] Sachet Singh and Sooraj Sharma, 'Investor-State Dispute Settlement Mechanism: The Quest For A Workable Roadmap' (2013) 29 Utrecht Journal of International and European Law 88, 92.

[33] 'Multinationals have exploited woolly definitions of expropriation to claim compensation for changes in government policy that happen to have harmed their business via ISDS' The Economist, 'The Arbitration Game' *The Economist* (2014) < http://www.economist.com/news/finance-and-economics/21623756-governments-are-souring-treaties-protect-foreign-investors-arbitration > accessed 12 December 2014.

[34] EurActiv | EU News & policy debates, across languages, 'ISDS Clause: A Gateway to Future Trade Deals' (9 December 2014) <http://www.euractiv.com/sections/ttip-and-arbitration-clause/isds-clause-gateway-future-trade-deals-310648> accessed 12 December 2014.

[35] See Corporate Europe Observatory, 'Still Not Loving ISDS: 10 Reasons To Oppose Investors' Super-Rights In EU Trade Deals' (*Corporate Europe,* 16 April 2014) < http://corporateeurope.org/international-trade/2014/04/still-not-loving-isds-10-reasons-oppose-investors-super-rights-eu-trade > accessed 12 December 2014.

[36] See Donald Robertson, 'Australia Goes against the Trend with Investor-State Dispute Settlement' (*FreeHills*, 20 May 2014) < http://www.herbertsmithfreehills.com/-/media/Freehills/Australia%20goes%20against%20the%20trend%20with.PDF > accessed 12 December 2014.

[37] M Sornarajah, *The International Law on Foreign Investment* (Cambridge University Press 2004), 202, para 2.

clauses violate this principle as it grants the foreign investors special rights to go to a third party tribunal whereas the domestic investors are unable to.[38] This argument is countered by the notion that the domestic investors have a better chance to get fair remedy in the domestic courts in case of an investment dispute. However the mere fact that foreign investors have a procedural mechanism in hand that the domestic investors do not, constitutes discrimination. In addition, examples of many BIT's show that countries are providing greater property protection to alien investors than the ones provided in their constitution.[39] For example the law in Germany does not provide for compensation to be paid in case of indirect expropriation but under the BIT's they are not exempted.[40] Several decisions by ISDS tribunals affirm that there is a trend of corporate restructuring in order to avail such special rights under a BIT.[41] It is also constantly criticized that ISDS mechanism is a one-sided process for example only the investors can sue to enforce rights.[42] The same liberality is not given to the host country government in case of bad acts from the investors.[43]

3.2. The Case of Regulatory Chill

Dr. Tietje promptly defines regulatory chill as, 'a State actor will fail to enact or enforce bona fide regulatory measures because of a perceived or actual threat of investment arbitration.'[44] So, instead of acting as a defender for the investors, the ISDS mechanism has become a weapon for them to defer, weaken or destroy regulation.[45] Therefore an increasing number of regulations are facing ISDS challenges which impede a sovereign's right to regulate.[46] The arguments against regulatory chill are that it is too difficult to prove and the ISDS mechanism has no right to annul the legislation.[47] Nonetheless there have been cases where threat of arbitration was a probable factor in a

---

[38] Ikenson, para 27.

[39] Corporate Europe Observatory, para 12.

[40] Ibid.

[41] UNCTAD (n9) 15.

[42] 'Investor State Dispute Settlement: A Sequel, UNCTAD Series on Issues in International Investment Agreements II (United Nations 2014), 115, para 2 < http://unctad.org/en/PublicationsLibrary/diaeia2013d2_en.pdf > accessed 12 December 2014.

[43] Corporate Europe Observatory, para 20.

[44] Tietje, 40, para 68.

[45] Kyla Tienhaara, 'Regulatory Chill and the Threat of Arbitration: A View from Political Science' [2010] Social Science Research Network, 3-4.

[46] Ikenson, para 29.

[47] Tietje, para 79.

country's choice to not enforce environmentally sensitive legislation[48], and a circumstance in which a country has decided to stand by its environmental policy[49] , which is therefore is now facing potentially serious consequences.[50]

3.3. The question of Transparency

The facts are that parties are not only permitted to choose the forum, they can further choose the law that governs the dispute and also the arbitrators, leading to what Professor Rogers calls 'Ultimate forum shopping'.[51] She further states:

> …The most important information sought is about the arbitrator's case management skills, approach to particular procedural or substantive issues and general professional style, information that published awards and law review articles are unlikely to reveal. In selecting an arbitrator, the elite international law firms and large corporations with extensive experience in international arbitration typically have a significant advantage.[52]

Furthermore the temporary tribunals are not bound to follow the decisions made by other tribunals in similar circumstances, leading to inconsistent, unpredictable outcomes.[53] In addition to this, the arbitrators are paid by the hour, making them interpret treaties expansively and giving them little incentive to adjudicate matter swiftly.[54]Lastly even though measures have been taken to disclose information regarding an ISDS proceeding, it can still be kept confidential if a party wants, making the process less transparent and hushed.[55]

---

[48] See the case of Indonesia and its Open pit mines at P. Jepson (2001) Science< https://www.sciencemag.org/content/292/5518/859.full > accessed on 12 December 2014.

[49] See Pac Rim Cayman LLC v. Republic of El Salvador on < http://icsidreview.oxfordjournals.org/content/28/1/15.short > accessed on 12 December 2014.

[50] Julia G. Brown, 'International Investment Agreements: Regulatory Chill In The Face Of Litigious Heat?' (2014) 3 Western Journal of Legal Studies 1, 18.

[51] Catherine A. Rogers, 'The Selection of Arbitrators in Investment Arbitration' (Organization of Economic Cooperation and Development (OECD) 2012), 4.<http://www.oecd.org/daf/inv/investment-policy/50241347.pdf > accessed 12 December 2014.

[52] Ibid.

[53] Lazo, 593, para 5.

[54] *The Economist*, para 5.

[55] Lazo, 593-594.

4. A CRITICAL ANALYSIS OF THE COMMONLY PROPOSED REFORMS

As the use of ISDS mechanisms increased exponentially over the last few decades, so have the criticisms of the mechanism.[56] The most common criticisms have been discussed above. In response to the criticisms, on 26 June 2013, the UNCTAD published a report proposing reforms to improve the existing international system for settling disputes between foreign investors and States (Hereinafter called UNCTAD Report 2013).[57] This section will evaluate the common reforms recommended to save the ISDS system, keeping in focus the ones suggested by UNCTAD.

4.1. Encouraging Other Methods of Alternative Dispute Solutions

TUNCTAD's report 2013 suggests that promotion of Alternative Dispute Resolution (ADR) methods such as mediation and conciliation[58], along with Dispute Prevention Policies (DPP), can effectively decrease the number of disputes that go into arbitration.[59] These methods do not include the strict application of legal rules and obligations, but instead focus on finding a harmonious solution to the problem with the help of a third party.[60] This consequently saves time, cost and also preserves the working relationships between the state and the investor.

The report however fails to mention how to successfully implement the idea. Almost all BITs include language encouraging the amicable settlement of disputes.[61] Some even have mandatory provisions.[62] However the UNCTAD 2010 report states that, "Despite the existence of rules and facilities

[56] "The total number of known treaty-based cases reached 568 by the end of 2013". See UNCTAD, 7.

[57] UNCTAD, 'Reform of Investor-State Dispute Settlement: In Search of a Roadmap' (United Nations 2013) 4-10 < http://unctad.org/en/PublicationsLibrary/webdiaepcb2013d4_en.pdf > accessed 13 December 2014, hereinafter called the UNCTAD Report 2013.

[58] For further information See the Mediation and conciliation Process: Key features, UNCATD, 'Investor–State Disputes: Prevention And Alternatives To Arbitration' (United Nations 2010) 28-29 < http://unctad.org/en/docs/diaeia200911_en.pdf > accessed 13 December 2014.

[59] UNCTAD 2013, 5.

[60] Herbert Smith Freehills - Arbitration notes, 'UNCTAD Proposes ISDS Reforms' (2013) < http://hsfnotes.com/arbitration/2013/07/15/unctad-proposes-isds-reforms/ > accessed 13 December 2014.

[61] Tietje, para 204. Also see for example, Article 10(14) of the US-Chile FTA; Article 88 of the Japan-Chile FTA; Article 11(15) of the Korea-Australia FTA.

[62] See Economic Partnership Agreement (EPA) between Japan and the Republic of Indonesia of 2007, Article 9 of the BIT between India and Sweden of 2000, Article 23 of the United States Model BIT of 2004.

dealing with conciliation and mediation procedures, their application in the investor–State context have to date been minimal"[63] . There are no statistics available to prove that the situation has improved. Moreover, the ADR and DPP mechanism is based on the foundation that the parties will cooperate but such so-operation might be difficult to achieve in the advent of a dispute. Also there might be bureaucratic hindrance, no access to a qualified neutral mediator and legally unenforceable solutions leading to wastage of time and money if the process fails to bring solution acceptable to both the parties.[64] Lastly, it fails to solve the problem of transparency as the ADR processes are also confidential.

4.2. Modifying the Prevailing System

This proposal consists of bringing about modification to certain aspects of ISDS mechanism. This mostly includes procedural innovations such as limitation clauses to bringing claim, power of interpretation of certain parts of the treaty by the parties themselves, consolidation of claims, allowing public access to dispute documents and hearing and speedy disposal of frivolous claims.[65]The advantage to this modification is that it is very easy to implement as only few parties are involved, two in the case of BITs and furthermore the parties can choose which issues to address.[66]

However, the effectiveness of this reform is questionable. The UNCTAD 2013 report mentions that applying this approach warrants renegotiation of the old IIA's.[67] Considering how difficult it is to enter into treaties, the parties might not want to go through the process of renegotiation once a treaty is already made. Moreover, the introduction of limitation clause is nothing new. Many treaties such as the 1992 North American Free Trade Association Treaty , the Canada-Czech Republic BIT (1992), AFTA (2004), NAFTA (1992), the Investment Agreement for the COMESA Common Investment Area (2007) and the ASEAN Comprehensive Investment Agreement (2009) has limitation periods.[68] This did not reduce the amount of cases that were filed. For example 49 claims were filed using NAFTA (which had a limitation clause) and 29 claims were filed under Energy Charter Treaty that did not

---

[63] UNCTAD 2010, 61.
[64] Mark A. Clodfelter, 'Why Aren'T More Investor-State Treaty Disputes Settled Amicably?' (United Nations Publications 2011) 38, 40 < http://unctad.org/en/docs/webdiaeia20108_en.pdf > accessed 13 December 2014.
[65] UNCTAD Report 2013, 6.
[66] Ibid., 7.
[67] Ibid.
[68] Paul, Mashiago, and Nohan, 22.

have a limitation clause.[69] With respect to the consolidation of claims, the host State might hope that at least one of the claimants will not press its claim or that, strategically, if the proceedings remain separate, it would have a better chance of winning in at least one of them.[70]

Granting the parties' power to interpret after a dispute might not work as well as there might be conflict of interpretation resulting into unnecessary delay. Encouraging transparency through public access to information and dispute hearing, along with allowing non-party civil organization to participate on the proceedings is a brilliant idea. The only problem it imposes is how then the Arbitration Tribunal is supposed to protect the confidential business information of the investor's business.[71] This reformation to procedural mechanism is thus very patchy and fails to achieve a comprehensive approach to the way forward.[72]

4.3. Restraining Investors' Access to ISDS

The reformation scheme suggests that the States could revise the scope of their consent to arbitration in future treaties by (i) reducing the subject matter of ISDS claims; (ii) restricting the range of investors who qualify to bring claims, or (iii) introducing a requirement to exhaust local remedies before resorting to international arbitration.[73] By limiting the scope of ISDS subject matter to some exhaustive concepts like "direct expropriation", by properly defining what investment is and by introducing provisions like mandatory exhaustion of domestic remedies, it can be hoped that there will be a considerable decrease in instituting ISDS claims.[74]

Nevertheless, there are some faults in these measures. Even if parties settle for a narrow scope to subject-matter of ISDS claim they can still launch claim using the broad interpretation of 'Umbrella clauses'[75] provisions. The 'Salini

---

[69] UNCTAD, 'Recent Development in Investor State Dispute Settlement' (United Nations May 2013)2 < http://unctad.org/en/PublicationsLibrary/webdiaepcb2013d3_en.pdf > accessed 13 December 2014.

[70] UNCTAD 2013(n16) 111. Also see CME/Lauder dispute, the Czech Republic refused to consent to the consolidation of the two cases, as proposed by the claimants, and prevailed in one of the cases. Key Cases From2000–2010 (1st edn, IISD) 34 < http://www.iisd.org/pdf/2011/int_investment_law_and_sd_key_cases_2010.pdf > accessed 13 December 2014.

[71] UNCTAD, 'Transparency' (United Nations 2012), 37, para 4 < http://unctad.org/en/PublicationsLibrary/unctaddiaeia2011d6_en.pdf > accessed 13 December 2014.

[72] Herbert Smith Freehills - Arbitration notes.

[73] UNCTAD Report 2013, 7, para 1.

[74] Ibid., 7-8.

[75] "An umbrella is a provision in an international investment agreement (IIA) by which the host state guarantees the observation of obligations assumed by it with respect to investments"

criteria'[76] of defining investment or investors , which itself is quite a broad one of defining investment is a debatable one rejected by many tribunals.[77] The requirement of exhausting local remedies before international arbitration might again lead to issues of politicization and discrimination. The foreign investors are most likely to be dissatisfied by its decision, thus ultimately resorting to ISDS but wasting resources like time and money while doing so.[78]

4.4. Introducing an Appeals Facility

Creating a central appellate system is a possible means of improving consistency among awards and enhancing predictability reducing some of the legitimacy concerns of the current regime.[79] It seems attainable if constituted of permanent members, appointed by States from a pool of the most reputable jurists.[80] However, the UNCTAD report also raised several important structural questions: Would the facility be implemented as an amendment to the ICSID Convention, and therefore limited in scope to ICSID awards? How would members be appointed, and for what duration? How would it be financed? What would be the scope of review? [81]

Even if the implementation of the appeals facility is achieved as many countries are now considering it[82], there are other clear issues. For example, it is contrary to the principle of finality i.e. that an arbitration award is binding and not open to appeal on the merits (a major advantage of ISDS mechanism).[83] Moreover, it will also be time consuming and costly , not to mention the enormous loads of cases the appellate facility will be burdened with.[84] Although this reform might lead to consistency of decisions which will be difficult considering that each case is dependent on an individual treaty. It will not solve the problem of the caseload .

---

see Dr. Alexander Shchavelev, 'Umbrella Clauses. A Balanced Approach to Interpretation' (Grin.com, 2012) < http://www.grin.com/en/e-book/262674/umbrella-clauses-a-balanced-approach-to-interpretation > accessed 14 December 2014.

[76] The criteria were formulated in Salini Costruttori S.p.A. and Italstrade S.p.A. v. Kingdom of Morocco (ICSID Case No. ARB/00/4), Decision on Jurisdiction, 31 July 2001.

[77] UNCTAD 2013, 12.

[78] Tietje, para 195.

[79] UNCTAD Report 2013, 8.

[80] Ibid.

[81] Ibid., 9.

[82] Katia Yannaca-small, 'Improving the System of Investor-State Dispute Settlement' (OECD Publishing 2006)9-10 < http://www.oecd.org/china/WP-2006_1.pdf > accessed 14 December 2014.

[83] Nicolette Butler, 'Possible Improvements to the Framework of International Investment Arbitration' (2013) 14 Journal of World Investment & Trade, 613, 634.

[84] Ibid., 635.

4.5.Creating a Permanent International Investment Court

This proposal goes hand in hand with the above recommendation of having an appellate mechanism. The UNCTAD 2013 report suggests replacement of the current system of temporary arbitral tribunals with a dedicated international court to hear investment disputes.[85] Aiding to the interests of investors, other concerned stakeholders and the state, a standing investment court would be institution of public welfare.[86] It is by far the best solution to the inconsistency and erroneous decision problem and is also the one which is most challenging to implement.[87]

Apart from the issue of implementation any centralized dispute resolution institution would continue to have a legitimacy crisis as the states might not be happy with the institution's jurisdictional power.[88] In addition even though supporters might argue that having a permanent court with permanently appointed judges solves the problems of undue incentives and systematic bias of the arbitrators, this issue is questionable.[89] For example there might be other reasons for expansive interpretations of treaty such as that is how arbitrators view their role, or there is no guarantee that permanently appointed judges will not have an issue of politicization.[90]

5. ISDS: A ROAD TO RECOVERY

Even though the abovementioned recommendations have their limitations, they are still viable solutions. It fails to solve some of the major problems of the ISDS such as granting superior rights to investors and questions of sovereign rights of the states. Amidst all the challenges that ISDS mechanism faces it is very important to remember that ISDS is merely a procedural enforcement mechanism for substantive commitment made by the parties in the respective IIAs.[91] Thus the responsibility of reforming the system should be divided into two parts: The parties making the substantive rules i.e. the state parties to the treaty and the one enforcing the rules i.e. the international forums of arbitration[92] mainly using ICSID and UNICITRAL rules.

---

[85] UNCTAD Report 2013(n57) 9.
[86] Ibid.
[87] Herbert Smith Freehills - Arbitration notes.
[88] European Parliamentary Report, 'Investor-State Dispute Settlement (ISDS) State Of Play and Prospects for Reform' (European Parliamentary Research Support 2014), 9.
[89] Catherine A. Rogers, 'The Politics of International Investment Arbitrators' (2014) 12 Santa Clara Journal of International Law 225, 249.
[90] Ibid., 250.
[91] UNCTAD 2014, 170, para 2.
[92] Tuck, 885.

5.1. Responsibilities of the State Parties to Treaties

It has been often argued that ambiguous provisions of the treaty has given the arbitrators more power with regard to interpretation thus leading to erroneous decisions.[93] The state parties should be accountable to draft treaties with clarifying key ideas and provisions, cautiously defining the scope of the treaties, alongside clear ISDS clauses.[94]

The first and foremost provision that is to be drafted comprehensively or exhaustively is the definition clause of 'Investment'. The non-exhaustive definition of this term has been one of the lead questions in many ISDS cases.[95] Some recent treaties, for example Article 11.28 in Australia/Korea BIT 2013 have incorporated exhaustive definitions of these terms.[96] A denial of benefit clause should be added as a precautionary measure to prevent treaty-shopping.[97] As the tribunal in Tidewater v. Venezuela noted, 'restructuring investments only in order to gain jurisdiction under a BIT would constitute an abusive manipulation of the system of international investment protection'.[98] This feature would potentially discourage assess to the treaty by corporate restructuring.

Another significant question that arises is about the balance between the private right of foreign investors and states right to making public policies.[99] This can be done by increasing exclusion clauses. Many IIAs eliminate regulation of financial services and taxation rules.[100]The state parties can be protected from potential ISDS claims by extending their right to regulate in case of public issues like environment, health, compliance with law, protection of national treasures, conservation of natural resources and labor in

---

[93] R.S. French AC, 'Investor-State Dispute Settlement — A Cut above the Courts?' International Trade Law Symposium (Law Council of Australia 2014) 2 < http://www.lawcouncil.asn.au/ILS/images/2014%20International%20Trade%20Law%20Symposium%20Papers%20-%20FINAL.pdf > accessed 14 December 2014.

[94] Reinisch, 26.

[95] UNCTAD 2013, 12.

[96] Hilary Birks and Anna MacMohan, 'Allens: Publication: Focus: Investor-State Dispute Settlement Under The Korea-Australia Free Trade Agreement' (Allens.com.au, 2014) < http://www.allens.com.au/pubs/ibo/foibo6mar14.htm#KAFTA > accessed 14 December 2014.

[97] Article 2, Canada and US model BIT, Marie-France Houde, 'Novel Features In Recent OECD Bilateral Investment Treaties' (OECD Directorate for Financial and Enterprise Affairs 2006) 144, 150 < http://www.oecd.org/daf/inv/internationalinvestmentagreements/40072428.pdf > accessed 15 December 2014.

[98] *Tidewater vs Venezuela* ICSID Case No ARB/10/5, para 150 < http://www.italaw.com/sites/default/files/case-documents/italaw1277.pdf > accessed 15 December 2014.

[99] Hinderlang, 113.

[100] Tietje, para 211.

their exclusion clause.[101] A study by Abbot, Erixon and Ferracane in 2014 found that among 90 cases that were concluded between 2003-2013, in six known cases the investor had complained about direct expropriation , and in 15 cases the investor complained of indirect expropriation.[102] So parties can narrow the dispute settlement cases by limiting it to direct expropriation like some treaties of China and Russia or specify a scope for indirect expropriation.[103]

Vague provisions such as 'minimum standard of treatment' or the 'umbrella clause' should be excluded from treaties to avoid long-shot potential claims.[104] Instead the minimum standard of treatment can be identified in detailed clauses as can be seen in article 3.2 of Central America Free Trade Agreement (CAFTA).[105] It is important to consider that there is a tendency of investors to overcome the narrow clauses by resorting to the most-favored-nation clauses (MFN clauses).[106] A MFN clause, as defined by UNCTAD , requires a State to grant investors covered by the IIA, treatment no less favorable than it has accorded to investors from any third country.[107] This is clearly a way of importing new substantive standard from other treaties.[108] There have been instances where arbitration tribunals overcame narrow clauses with this provision.[109] So it is perhaps wise for parties to exclude launching claim in ISDS using MFN clause.

Lastly, the obligation by the host state to provide fair and equitable treatment (FET) often leads to inconsistent interpretation by tribunals.[110] Most BIT and IIA in the past doesn't elaborate its meaning and thus it is left to the Arbitration Tribunal to specify whether an act violates the provision of FET.[111] So the state should limit the scope of such obligation in order avoid ISDS claims. For example of article 5 of US model BIT which specifies FET

---

[101] Birks and MacMohan.

[102] Roderick Abbott, Fredrik Erixon and Martina Ferracane, 'Demystifying Investor-State Dispute Settlement (ISDS)' (2014) 5 *ECIPE Occasional Paper* 1, 14.

[103] A. Reinisch, 'How Narrow Are Narrow Dispute Settlement Clauses in Investment Treaties?' (2011) 2 Journal of International Dispute Settlement 1, 3.

[104] Brown, 19.

[105] Ibid.

[106] Reinisch, 17.

[107] UNCTAD 2014, 162.

[108] Kent.ac.uk, 'Statement Of Concern About Planned Provisions On Investment Protection And Investor-State Dispute Settlement (ISDS) In The Transatlantic Trade And Investment Partnership (TTIP) - Kent Law School - University Of Kent' (2014) < http://www.kent.ac.uk/law/isds_treaty_consultation.html > accessed 15 December 2014.

[109] A majority of the tribunal in Garanti Koza v. Turkmenistan agreed to apply the MFN clause to jurisdictional matters. See UNCTAD, 17.
For further information see Reinisch, 18-38.

[110] UNCTAD 2014, 27.

[111] Tietje, para 121.

should be equivalent to customary international law granting minimum standard of treatment of aliens.[112]

5.2. Responsibilities of the Arbitration Forums

Any determination to improve ISDS mechanism must include changes to the arbitrators who make up the ISDS tribunals. In order for arbitrators to be fair and devoid of undue incentives, the present system of temporary payment should be changed. They should be paid fixed salaries for fixed terms and be from diverse countries.[113] An OECD report states that over 50 percent of ISDS arbitrators have acted as counsel for investors in other ISDS cases while it has been estimated about 10 percent of ISDS arbitrators have acted as counsel for States in other cases[114], giving scope to criticism of issue conflicts. Having a permanent position could also solve the conflict of issues problem. The arbitrators could then be required to not take up the position of a counsel in any ISDS case during their tenure as a permanent arbitrator.[115] The number of arbitrators should also be increased and they should hear cases that they have no financial or other stake in.[116] There could be a nomination committee constituted under the ICSID and UNICTRAL rules to take care of the appointment, remuneration and conduct of the permanently appointed arbitrators.

However, acknowledging the fact that implementation of the idea of permanent arbitrators could take a long time, the parties perhaps could have a mutual list of selected arbitrators. In times of a dispute the arbitrators could be chosen from such list and thereby reducing the challenges to arbitrators and ensuring transparency. Although the recent reforms in both ICSID and UNICITRAL rules to increase transparency via disclosure of case information, allowing amicus curie briefs and disclosure of issue conflicts have been praiseworthy[117], it has to take into consideration the abovementioned recommendations. The arbitrators should also be required to follow precedents as much as applicable to resolve uncertainty.[118] The phrase

---

[112] Article 5, US Model BIT< http://www.ustr.gov/sites/default/files/BIT%20text%20for%20ACIEP%20Meeting.pdf> accessed 15 December 2014.

[113] Brown, 22.

[114] David Gaukrodger and Kathryn Gordon, "'Investor-State Dispute Settlement: A Scoping Paper for the Investment Policy Community' (OECD 2012) 44, para 2 < http://www.oecd.org/daf/inv/investment-policy/WP-2012_3.pdf> accessed 15 December 2014.

[115] UNCTAD 2014, 179-180.

[116] Ibid.

[117] Tuck.

[118] Brown, 6.

'as much as applicable' should be highlighted as it would be unfair to use precedent without such reservation due to cases being based on different treaties and the temporary nature of the tribunals.[119] There should be more emphasis given to establish a uniform code of conduct for the arbitrators.[120] For example the EU-Canada FTA has a binding code of conduct based on the ethical rules of the International Bar Association.[121]

6. CONCLUSION

Irrespective of the fact that the mentioned path to a future of ISDS in the paper is immensely difficult to implement, it is of necessity to do so. In the face of all the criticisms of the system it is very important to remember that ISDS provisions are based on basic principles of respect for private property and the rule of law. The protections were initially intended to prevent discrimination, repudiation of contracts, and expropriation of property without due process of law and just compensation.[122] The assurance of these protections is not a mere luxury but is essential to attract foreign investors which in turn brings economic development to states. However, there is also increased disapproval of the fact that these protections can sometimes impede the state's right to regulate on public policies.[123] It can be rectified by cooperation from both the state parties and the neutral arbitration forums as suggested in the paper. Thus states should help to avoid unnecessary litigation by drafting investment clauses as precise as possible, defining the scope of ISDS which will deter investors from bringing hopeless claims.[124] On the other hand the enforcement mechanism should be transparent, avoid inconsistent decision and deal with real issues of substantive investment laws.

---

[119] Ibid.

[120] Tietje, para 239.

[121] Stefan Rützel and Stephan Wilske, '07 European Union Overview Chapter - International Arbitration 2014' (International Comparative Legal Guides, 2014) < http://www.iclg.co.uk/practice-areas/international-arbitration-/international-arbitration-2014/european-union-overview > accessed 15 December 2014.

[122] Justthefacts.pmi.com, 'Trade Agreements and ISDS: Protecting Public Interest and Protectors – Just the Facts' (2014) < http://justthefacts.pmi.com/international-trade-agreements-and-isds-protecting-the-intellectual-property-rights-of-legal-business/ > accessed 15 December 2014.

[123] Brown, 24.

[124] August, 23.

Suing Public Authorities: Who Wins?

Tom Stafford[†]

This article argues that Civil Law is fundamentally unsuitable to dealing either with i) grievances against the way a Public Authority has handled a particular situation; or ii) loss that one has suffered at the hands of a public authority acting negligently. The rationale behind this conclusion is based on the belief that suing public bodies for negligence is problematic as it is an inordinately expensive process for the taxpayer and, being a fault-based system of liability, often leaves deserving individuals who have simply been the victims of bad luck with no compensation for their loss. Moreover, the state of the case law is doctrinally incoherent and unstable, and thus in need of re-examination.

Keywords: liability of public authorities, negligence, duty of care, public bodies, fault-based compensation, law reform, public liability, omissions liability.

1. Introduction

Many are familiar with the term 'litigation culture', a platitude so often bandied about by the tabloid press that seems determined to present a caricature of greedy, ambulance-chasing lawyers. In many cases this is an unfair portrayal; if someone has had their leg crushed in a warehouse accident because their employer neglected to follow basic health and safety legislation, then of course they should be compensated. As between individuals it is only right that wrongs should be remedied and any competent (or honest) lawyer will not advise his client to issue proceedings if there is little chance of success.

What is, on the other hand, rather disturbing, is the amount public authorities are spending on defending claims. Public money is supposed to be

[†] Paralegal at Clyde & Co LLP; Law BA, University of Cambridge.

directed towards the public good and it is alarming that so much of taxpayers' money is going directly into the pockets of lawyers. A recent report by MPs estimated that the National Health Service (NHS) is facing a £15.7 billion bill to settle an increasing number of Clinical Negligence claims[1] and this number is only increasing.

Of course, no-one is arguing that individuals who have suffered loss at the hands of well-meaning but negligent healthcare professionals should go away empty-handed, but what is frustrating about the figure is that most of those costs will have gone into the litigation battle itself[2] rather than to the actual victims.

Furthermore, the £15.7 billion quoted relates only to medical claims. Numerous arms of the public sector, including education authorities[3] and the police force[4] have to foot an enormous claims bill each year.

This state of affairs prompts the obvious question: who wins? Clearly it is not the taxpayer, nor the frontline service workers who go about their jobs with the constant threat of litigation hanging over their heads. And do those injured even benefit? Litigating is not a pleasant process; it is expensive, time consuming, and may not even lead to compensation. In reality the only winners are the lawyers. Medical negligence law, to take one illustrative example, can be an extremely lucrative practice area. One could be forgiven for tentatively suggesting that this area is perhaps more beneficial to those who practice it than to those they represent.

This article argues that Civil Law is a blunt instrument in this context, ill-equipped to deal with situations where something goes wrong with the provision of a public service. It will further be argued that when a claimant sues a public body, it is almost always for one of two reasons:

1. They have suffered a loss that needs compensating; or

---

[1] Murray Wardrop, 'NHS facing £15.7bn for rising number of clinical negligence claims' (*The Telegraph*, 7 February 2012) < http://www.telegraph.co.uk/news/politics/9065534/NHS-facing-15.7bn-for-rising-number-of-clinical-negligence-claims.html > accessed 5 September 2015.

[2] Action Against Medical Accidents, *AVMA Action Against Medical Accidents Response to Welsh Assembly Consultation on Proposed NHS Redress (Wales) Measure* (Response, September 2007) < http://www.assembly.wales/NAfW%20Documents/nhsr19_-_action_against_medical_accidents_140907.pdf%20-%2024092007/nhsr19_-_action_against_medical_accidents_140907-English.pdf > accessed 5 September 2015

[3] Lord Hoffmann, *Reforming the Law of Public Authority Negligence* (Bar Council Law Reform Lecture 2009) < http://www.barcouncil.org.uk/media/100362/lord_hoffmann_s_transcript_171109.pdf > accessed 5 September 2015.

[4] Rebecca Café, 'Metropolitan Police spends £9m in six years on compensation' (*BBC News*, 12 May 2012) < http://www.bbc.com/news/uk-england-london-18021317 > accessed 5 September 2015.

2. They feel aggrieved as a result of malpractice and would like to see those responsible held accountable, and maybe prevent such mistakes from reoccurring.

Negligence liability achieves both these aims, but only to an inadequate extent. In relation to compensating loss, this is of course one of the key purposes of tort law. However, as with any system of fault-based liability, the claimant only receives compensation if she can establish fault. This leaves a huge lacuna in the system for those who have suffered loss that was neither their fault nor the result of bad practices, but just an unfortunate accident. Under the current system they may have to spend large amounts of money suing public authorities and in the end not even receive compensation for their loss. Alternatively, if someone feels aggrieved by the way they were treated by a member belonging to a public body, they may litigate to seek redress. Whilst they may feel vindicated if successful and those involved in the malpractice *may* be disciplined for their actions, there is no guarantee of this, and equally no mechanism in place to ensure that future practices are improved.

The answer, it is suggested, is to deal with these two aims separately, and to establish different mechanisms, one for compensation and one for holding public bodies to account.

2. Historical Foundations

To some extent, our current state of affairs is a product of the evolution of English Common Law. It can be traced back to the rule formulated by *Dicey*, that the Crown should be under the same responsibilities as the ordinary citizen. As put by *Dicey* himself:

> In England ... every official, from the Prime Minister down to a constable or a collector of taxes, is under the same responsibility for every act done without legal justification as any other citizen.[5]

The sentiment behind this rule is admirable. It was to ensure the accountability of government and to stop officials enjoying any special privileges or immunities, which is of course a cornerstone of the essence of rule of law. The rule was largely a reaction to the system of French Public Law which prevailed at the time, under which the authorities were answerable

[5] Albert Venn Dicey, *Introduction to the Study of the Law of the Constitution* (5th edn, Macmillan 2009).

to ordinary citizens through a different set of rules (this in reality allowed the government to function above the law). Nevertheless, the *Diceyean* rule worked extremely well, as it meant that any act which would be illegal for an ordinary citizen to commit was equally illegal when committed by an employee of a government institution. To take a celebrated example, in *Entick v Carrington*[6] the King's servants broke into the plaintiff's house, who was rumoured to be the author of seditious writings, armed with a warrant from the Secretary of State. Under the Common Law this amounted to trespass, and the defence founded on the warrant was not even briefly entertained by Lord Camden CJ.

At the time, the rule that the State should be liable for the same wrongs as its citizens was perfectly desirable and made absolute sense. However there have been a couple of developments, one legal and one social which have cumulatively muddied the waters since.

The first is the expansion of the State. In the 20th Century the State has come to regulate far more aspects of citizens' lives than in the 18th Century. In Dicey's day, the main reason an individual would bring a suit against the government was because it had committed some illegal act, such as trespass. However, as the State has come to regulate more and more of aspects of our daily lives, it is easier to attribute blame to it. Atiyah writes:

> If the public thinks – as some people seem to think – that ultimately the government is responsible for everything that happens in society, then the government (and other public bodies) are liable to get sued, whatever they do or fail to do. [7]

It is a fact of modern society that because the Government's responsibilities are so wide ranging, one can plausibly blame the government for any badly kept road, E-coli outbreak, or criminal attack that could have feasibly been prevented.

The second development is legal, and is the birth of the *duty of care* in Tort. *Donoghue v Stevenson*[8] was a watershed case in English Law in that it saw the establishment of the duty of care, which has become the cornerstone of the law of negligence. The admission that one may actually be under a duty in certain circumstances to *prevent* harm occurring to another person has become central in establishing tortious liability. Between ordinary citizens, there usually has to be some proximity or reason for the imposition of this duty. For example, the defendant has created the dangerous situation which harms the claimant, as was the case in *Donoghue*. However, with the

---

[6] *Entick v Carrington* [1765] EWHC KB J98 (Westminster Hall).
[7] P. S. Atiyah, *The Damages Lottery* (Hart Publishing, 1997), 139.
[8] *Donoghue v Stevenson* [1932] UKHL 100 [1932] AC 562.

expansion of the State it could be argued, and often is, that the Government has a constant duty of care over its citizens.

That leaves us with our situation today. We have a law of negligence that is framed around the concept of the duty of care, which means that, unlike in the 18th century, the government does not have to actively commit a wrongful act to be sued. We have seen a sharp increase in litigation against public bodies over the last few decades which is showing very little sign of slowing down.

3. Why Civil Law Has Failed as a Means of Redress Against Public Bodies

There are a number of reasons why the current case-law on the civil liability of public bodies is deeply flawed. It is incoherent, as it is often is at odds with public law; it is constantly evolving, with cases often departing from the *ratio decidendi* of previous decisions resulting legal certainty; it has proven to be incredibly difficult in the context of omissions liability; it can be overly restrictive and often leaves individuals without any form of redress at all. Above all, it is leaves an enormous bill to be picked up by the taxpayer.

3.1. The Contradictory and Unstable Nature of the Law

The relationship between public law and the civil liability of public bodies has always been difficult. The classic rule was that it was not possible to conjure up a common law duty of care from a statutory power. The question was always whether the statute in question *excludes* a duty of care. As was put by Lord Steyn in *Gorringe v Calderdale*[9]:

> … in a case framed in Negligence, against the background of a statutory duty or power, a basic question is whether the statute *excludes* a private law remedy?[10]

This does not fit well with public law at all. The controlling concept in public law is whether, by reference to Parliamentary intent, the statutory power exercised was *intra vires* (lawful) or *ultra vires* (unlawful). It is anomalous that a claimant can bring two suits: a claim in negligence and a judicial review, and that the action could be found to be illegal, yet immune from a civil suit.

---

[9] *Gorringe v Calderdale MBC* [2004] UKHL 14, [2004] 1 WLR 1057.

[10] *Gorringe,* para 3.

For a while, in an attempt to maintain some coherence between public and private law, the courts did try to import the public law test of *Wednesbury Unreasonableness* into the Civil Law at stage 3 of the *Caparo* test[11] in deciding whether it would be 'fair just and reasonable' to impose a duty of care. However, this practice has since been jettisoned. As put by Lord Hutton in *Barrett v Enfield Borough Council*[12]:

> [I]t is preferable for the courts to decide the validity of the plaintiff's claim by applying directly the common law concept of Negligence than by applying as a preliminary test the public law concept of Wednesbury unreasonableness…to determine if the decision fell outside the ambit of the statutory discretion[13]

In light of this there is no longer any symmetry required between the public and civil law when it comes to the lawfulness action taken by public authorities.

3.2. Suing Public Bodies Has Been Particularly Difficult in the Context of Omissions Liability

The classic rule in English law is that a defendant cannot be held responsible for their own omissions unless they were under a specific duty to act. As stated above, public bodies could in theory be said to be under a duty to act in almost every situation. Therefore, what is an appropriate rule between individuals does not lend itself to cases between the individual and the State.

This has in the past even led to unfairness. For example, in *East Suffolk Rivers Catchment Board v. Kent*[14], a farmer's field was flooded by a river bursting its banks. The local authority decided to repair the banks of the river. This took years rather than months, and Kent the farmer was unable to use his land, which led to a marked loss of earnings. He sued for negligence and his claim was rejected by the House of Lords, who held that the action was based on the fallacy that the authorities were under an obligation to act in the first place, which they weren't:

> It is admitted that the respondents would have no claim if the appellants had never intervened at all. In my opinion, the respondents equally have no claim when the appellants do

[11] *Caparo Industries plc v Dickman* [1990] UKHL 2, [1990] 2 AC 605.
[12] *Barrett v Enfield Borough Council* [2001] 2 AC 550 (HL).
[13] *Barrett*, 586.
[14] *East Suffolk Rivers Catchment Board v Kent* [1941] AC 71 (HL).

> intervene, save in respect of such damage as flows from their intervention and as might have been avoided if their intervention had been more skilfully conducted.[15]

This does seem like quite a hard rule when employed in this context. One could argue on the facts that the case was wrongly decided, as the authority had intervened, but in an unsatisfactory manner. However, even when under different facts, if the local authorities had decided money could be better spent elsewhere, it does seem somewhat unfair that this benefit to society as a whole should be borne by one individual.

Conversely there are cases where the rule could be considered a potentially useful guard against floods of litigation. For example, compensation was denied to the claimant in *Stovin v. Wise*[16]. Here, there was a dangerous embankment near a junction which had caused a number of accidents. The Council knew of this and had planned to remove it. However, in the meantime Stovin, the claimant, had suffered an accident at the junction and the defendant, Wise, claimed that the Council were partially to blame. Fortunately, this was dismissed by the majority in the House of Lords.

In short, whilst it can sometimes achieve desirable results, the no-liability-for-omissions rule, which serves an extremely useful purpose in suits between individuals, has proven to be somewhat useless in actions between individuals and public bodies.

3.3. An Overly Restrictive System

Another key problem with the current system, closely linked to the previous point, is that it often leaves individuals with no redress in cases where it at least intuitively feels that some should be available.

The latest House of Lords leading case on public authorities' civil liability is *Gorringe*.[17] Though this decision did not receive a particularly strong reaction from commentators it did in fact change the rules quite radically.

On the facts, the decision was absolutely correct: Mrs Gorringe was driving round a bend too fast, lost control of her car and crashed into a bus. She then sued the local authority because the word "slow" used to be painted at the bend and wasn't anymore. Gorringe sued on the basis that there was a statutory duty to prepare and carry out a programme of measures to promote road safety, which she submitted generated a parallel common law duty. Clearly it would have been absurd if she had been able to recover damages.

---

[15] *East Suffolk Rivers*, 88.
[16] *Stovin v Wise* (Norfolk CC, Third Party) [1996] AC 923 (HL).
[17] *Gorringe*.

However, the way in which the House of Lords limited liability was problematic. Arguably, it would have been simpler to find there was a duty, but deny damages at the causation stage, as the claimant was clearly responsible for her own misfortune. Instead, Lord Hoffmann said that he found it:

> ... difficult to imagine a case in which a common law duty [could] be founded simply upon the failure (however irrational) to provide some benefit which a public authority has power (or a public law duty) to provide.[18]

Previously the rule had simply been that there was no private law duty on a public law power. As pointed out in *The liability of public authorities for failing to confer benefits*[19] this was quite a radical development from *Stovin v Wise*[20], as Nolan points out:

> There can be no doubt that *Gorringe* was a very restrictive decision. Whereas the majority in *Stovin* limited their analysis to the failure to exercise a statutory power, in *Gorringe* the House of Lords dealt both with the failure to exercise a statutory power and the failure to exercise a statutory *duty* [emphasis added].[21]

What is problematic about the ruling is that whilst the rule that Public Law duties can never generate a common law duty of care is useful when claimants like Mrs. Gorringe try to sue their local authority because they've crashed their car into a bus, there are equally cases in which a statutory duty to provide a service should in fact generate a common law duty of care. Statutory duties are often imposed on authorities to provide and care for vulnerable people in their care, for example, children in the custody of a governmental body, and it would seem strange if this type of statutory duty could never generate a duty of care.

3.4. The 'Assumption of Responsibility' Test Generates Arbitrary Results

Another problematic feature of the current law is the Courts' use of the 'assumption of responsibility' test as a means of limiting liability. Like the no-

---

[18] *Gorringe*; Lord Hoffmann (n 3) para [32].
[19] Donal Nolan, 'The liability of public authorities for failing to confer benefits' [2011] 127 LQR 260.
[20] *Stovin.*
[21] Nolan.

liability-for-omissions rule, this only really functions properly between individuals. Asking whether a local authority has 'assumed responsibility' for a situation is highly artificial, because as mentioned above, public bodies could be said to be responsible for any issue that falls within their remit.

In reality, the test, which works between individuals, is meaningless when one is dealing with a statutory body providing a service, and has just become an empty platitude which the courts hide behind when making intuition-based decisions.

This is illustrated when one contrasts two cases: *Kent v Griffiths*[22] and *Capital & Counties Plc. v Hampshire County Council*[23].

In *Kent v Griffiths* the claimant had an asthma attack and summoned an ambulance. The ambulance took forty minutes to arrive, during which time she had suffered a respiratory arrest. The ambulance service was held liable in negligence on that it had assumed responsibility for the claimant's safety.

In stark contrast, in *Capital & Counties*[24], a fire broke out in the claimants' building. The fire service arrived, turned off the sprinkler system and failed to effectively fight the fire, leading to excessive damage. However, it was held that they had not assumed responsibility for the fire and thus were not liable for the damage.

There is a lack of any intelligible factual difference between these cases, yet the fact that the court in each reached the opposite result illustrates the inadequacy of the 'assumption' test, and is further demonstrative of the wider unsuitability of the private law of negligence in claims against public bodies.

3.5. The Current System Is Incredibly Expensive for the Taxpayer

Aside from leading to undesirable results in individual cases, all these suits against public authorities cumulatively total up to an incredibly high bill.

This was pointed out by Lord Hoffmann in his *Bar Council Reform Lecture*[25]. He took as a case study *Phelps v Hillingdon London Borough Council*[26] in which the House of Lords held a local authority liable for failing to diagnose dyslexia in children. This led to a flood of litigation, often unsuccessful, as due to the nature of the cases causation and fault are both incredibly hard to establish. Lord Hoffmann puts it perfectly:

---

[22] *Kent v Griffiths* [2000] 2 WLR 1158 (CA).

[23] *Capital & Counties Plc. v Hampshire County Council* [1997] 3 WLR (CA).

[24] *Capital and Counties*.

[25] "Reforming the Law of Public Authority Negligence".

[26] *Phelps v Hillingdon London Borough Council* [2000] UKHL 47 [2001] 2 AC 619.

> ...so far as my researches were able to go, I could find only three cases in which such claims had succeeded and in those the amounts recovered were relatively trivial… In Leicester I was shown a huge air conditioned warehouse in which school records are now kept until the latest possible extension of the limitation period has expired. The costs of such an action are at least £500,000, funded by the local authority on one side and the State on the other. Emotions run high … [and] [w]hen the action fails, as it almost invariably does, they will feel that the system has let them down again.[27]

This perfectly captures the expense and futility of the current system. Anything which costs so much money, yet rarely leads to satisfied claimants is in need of serious overhaul. As things stand at the moment, huge amounts of public time and money are being diverted away from socially desirable ends in order to fight pointless cases. This does prompt the question, who is currently winning? The only plausible answer seems to be the lawyers collecting their avaricious brief fees at the courtesy of the Taxpayer.

4. Proposed Solutions

If the current system is unfit for purpose, what should replace it? If not under the Civil Law, then how should claims be dealt with?

The reason that litigation against public authorities has been such an unqualified disaster is that it is ill-equipped to tackle the reasons people sue in the first place. As suggested above, in almost every case where individuals sue a public body it is for one of two reasons. Either:

1. They have suffered an injury, or some other form of loss, and are looking for compensation; or
2. They believe a public body has acted poorly, and would like to hold them accountable for their actions, and maybe ensure that such practices are improved in the future.

The law of Negligence is not at-all suited to deal with the second reason, and whilst one of its key purposes is to ensure that individuals are compensated, this is contingent upon the fault of the defendant. This implies that if the defendant's fault cannot be established on the facts, then compensation is denied. These objectives are separate and should be treated as such.

---

[27] "Reforming the Law of Public Authority Negligence", 11-12.

4.1. A Victim-Orientated Compensation Scheme

Under the current system, let us assume the circumstances of the victim of an operation that goes wrong and is left paralyzed and needs to recoup his loss of earnings. The victim's only option is to issue a claim. However, assuming the surgeon did everything right and the accident in question was simply a case of bad luck, the victim will be denied compensation.

This feels both unsatisfactory and unfair. If a victim has suffered an accident that was not his/her fault, should there not be some mechanism in place for compensation?

It is proposed that we scrap fault-based liability for public authorities. Civil servants are charged with acting in the public good. Sometimes, accidents happen. However, a doctor who makes a mistake is hardly comparable to the reckless driver who knocks a cyclist off her bike. If public servants could go about their day without the threat of litigation constantly hanging over their heads, ever mindful of the evidential boxes they are required to tick should the situation lead to a claim, then they would be able to concentrate on doing their actual jobs.

Equally, if someone has been the victim of an accident or disaster, why should fault be the determining factor of whether they are compensated? Surely compensation should be provided on the basis of need, rather than whether or not the finger of blame can be successfully pointed at someone?

This suggestion is not that radical. 43 years ago New Zealand passed the *Accident Compensation Act 1972*[28]**.** The provisions of this law were far more wide-ranging than the current proposals and included actions between private citizens. In short, New Zealand effectively abolished negligence liability. The merits and demerits of this kind of wide-ranging change can be discussed at a later date. The salient point, however, is that no-fault compensation schemes can work.

It is argued that the controlling factor on whether to award or withhold compensation should be the fault of the claimant, rather than the defendant.

If we compare the results this system would produce on some of the previously discussed cases, and compare these with the actual results, the desirability of this system becomes clear.

Take *Kent*[29] for example. Kent was the victim of a natural disaster. Because of the no-liability-for-omissions rule, Kent was denied recover, after both parties had incurred considerable costs. However, under the proposed scheme, a commission would have been able to swiftly deal with Kent's claim, establishing that he was not at fault and was in need of compensation. If we change the facts slightly, and imagine that the local authority had

---

[28] Accident Compensation Act 1972 (NZ).

[29] *Kent* [1941].

decided that repairing the flood defenses was not worth the time and money it would cost, then it is argued that Kent should still receive some compensation. This type of case would be caught by the 'risk principle'. This is the theory that if a decision is taken in the public good, but some individuals suffer as a result, they should be compensated accordingly. It was summarised by Lord Nicholls in *Marcic v. Thames Water Utilities Ltd*[30]:

> If a single house is at risk of flooding by sewerage discharge once every five years, this may not justify the investment that would be needed to remove that risk. It does not follow, however, that it is just that the householder should receive no compensation for the damage done. The flooding is a consequence of the benefit that is provided to those making use of the system. It seems to us at least arguable that to strike a fair balance between the individual and the general community, those who pay to make use of a sewerage system should be charged sufficient to cover the cost of paying compensation to the minority who suffer damage as a consequence of the operation of the system.[31]

Surely this is correct. Let us also imagine that the proposed system had been in place when *Gorringe v Calderdal*[32] had been decided. Here, the question again would have been whether the accident was Mrs Gorringe's fault. It clearly was. She drove into a bus. She would of course be denied compensation.

Costs regularly outstrip damages. If there is an available system which costs less and compensates more deserving cases than under the present state of affairs then it would be idiotic not to implement it.[33]

4.2. Greater use of ombudsman to hold public bodies accountable

The other main reason people are likely to litigate against public bodies is that, rather than having suffered loss with financial consequences, they feel aggrieved by what they believe to be a mishandling of their case, and would like to see those involved held accountable.

---

[30] *Marcic v Thames Water Utilities Ltd* [2002] EWCA Civ 65 [2002] Q.B. 929.
[31] *Marcic* [2002], Lord Nicholls, para 113.
[32] *Gorringe* [2004].
[33] Of course, the actual cost of this system cannot be confirmed without further research, but it would certainly be worth investigating.

One of the seminal cases is *Hill v Chief Constable of West Yorkshire* [34], in which the mother of one of the victims of the "Yorkshire Ripper" sued West Yorkshire police for failing to catch the murderer promptly, thus leading to the death of her daughter. It seems highly unlikely that Mrs. Hill's primary aim in suing was to secure a cash windfall.

It is of paramount importance that our law has a mechanism for holding public bodies to account and improve future practices. However, the law of negligence is not set up to address these concerns. Tort law provides a mechanism by which blame can be apportioned for a specific wrong, and that wrong can be remedied with a financial reward. However, after the damages have been paid out, there are no mechanisms in place to actively prevent the same mistakes being made in the future, or, in the cases of gross negligence, for those involved to be removed from their post.

A negligence suit, due to our adversarial system, asks the wrong questions. It simply asks whether we can blame the defendant, and if so, how much they should have to pay. There is no deeper inquiry into what went wrong.

This is, however, exactly what an ombudsman enquiry can achieve. Ombudsman are equipped to carry out an inquisitorial investigation that can delve into deeper issues than those directly affecting the two parties to the case, and as such, are a much more effectual mechanism for ensuring the accountability of public bodies. The Law Commission, in Law Commission Consultation Paper No 187,[35] noted:

> …the ombudsman can undertake large scale investigations into systemic issues and make findings and recommendations that can effect widespread administrative change. As such, the ombudsmen can play a crucial role in improving administrative action to the benefit of both public bodies and claimants.[36]

This is something which is markedly lacking in a negligence hearing.

5. Conclusion

Implementing the above suggestions would constitute an enormous upheaval of our Legal System and certainly should not be undertaken lightly. However, the experience of both litigants and the local authorities who defend their claims underlines the serious need for reform. We currently have a system in which a public body could be found to have acted unlawfully in an ultra vires

[34] *Hill v Chief Constable of West Yorkshire* [1989] AC 53.

[35] Law Commission, *Administrative Redress: Public Bodies and Citizen* (Consultation Paper No 187, 2008).

[36] Law Com No 187, para 2.16.

sense, that is, gone beyond the legal scope of their power, but not be liable to pay its victims any compensation. Under the current regime, bodies whose only source of funds is the taxpayer's money are having to settle huge court bills each year and yet those who have merely been the victims of misfortune, or who do not have the access to the evidence necessary to establish fault are denied recompense. Furthermore, those who have well-founded grievances arising out of their treatment by a public body are forced to fit their complaint into a negligence claim for want of more suitable channels of redress. Clearly this state of affairs is far from ideal. As I have argued, the reason for suing a public body will, in almost every case, fall into two categories: tangible financial loss that requires compensating; or a personal conviction that one has been treated unfairly. Negligence is inadequate in either case, for the aforementioned reasons. As such, alternative systems for dealing with each separately, and their estimated cost, could prove a fertile line of enquiry for the Law Commission.

Corporate Social Responsibility: Here to Stay

Andreas Thrasyvoulou[†]

This article discusses the importance of Corporate Social Responsibility (CSR) in the modern world. The problems that led to the financial crisis will be assessed, as well as why the CSR has been left outside the substantial reforms currently taken by a number of companies and financial institutions. The importance of stakeholders will also be discussed and the stakeholder theory will be analysed, as this is a fundamental part of CSR. Both CSR and stakeholder theory are aspects of an organic theory that acts as a fundamental mechanism in the institution's development. Moreover, reference will also be made to various corporate scandals, the new Company Law Act 2006, the recent regulations published in 2014 and the ground-breaking India Companies Act. These will serve as strong examples, supporting the author's suggestion that CSR is not a fad whose time has come, but an important theory, which is slowly emerging as one of the fundamental principles of legislative reform. In the author's opinion, this is a huge development post-financial crisis. Furthermore, the author will attempt to prove that CSR is an important component, which will help the development of a corporate financial market less vulnerable to a future financial crisis

Keywords: Corporate Social Responsibility, Company Law Act 2006, India Companies Act

[†] LLM, Queen Mary University of London; LLB, University of Sussex.

1. INTRODUCTION

The only socially responsible duty for a corporation is to, "use its resources and engage in activities designed to increase its profits so long as it stays within the rules of the game, which is to say, engages in open and free competition without deception or fraud."[1] Friedman's controversial thesis did not survive the financial crisis of 2008. The economic crisis highlighted that, even when playing "by the rules of the game", corporations are able to find ways to use every legal authority they have in order to maximise their profits. This condition led to short-termism and excessive risk taking, and the various factors that could maintain long-term sustainability were disregarded. Governments could not keep up with the new ways corporations found to abuse their corporate power.[2] This abuse resulted in various scandals, especially post-2008, when the global financial market almost collapsed. There is strong evidence, which supports the argument that Corporate Social Responsibility (CSR) can act as a self-regulatory mechanism, and help fill the gaps of legislation.[3] In the author's estimations, it is also visible that Friedman's words "deception or fraud" can have a broader meaning, as it is not necessarily illegal, but may be ethically wrong, therefore running counter to the the foundations of CSR. This paper will explain terms such as the financial crisis of 2008 and CSR in more detail. The author will also consider the importance of the stakeholder theory post-2008 and the manner in which it overlaps with CSR, as well as how policies based on CSR and stakeholder consideration can have many benefits, such as long-term financial sustainability. In addition, the immense support that these policies are garnering from various NGOs, the European Union (EU), the United Nations along with other countries which will also be discussed, and the importance of this for the corporate field, since they possess a direct link to competitiveness and consequently capital maximisation. The author of the essay shares the suspicions of others that the crisis has "planted seeds for two new crises: rising government debt and inflation".[4] The paper will also explore the legislative reforms in UK; the Companies Act of 2006,[5] and the Enlightened

[1] Friedman, M., "VII Capitalism and discrimination" at page 112 in *Capitalism and Freedom; The classic statement of Milton Friedman's economic philosophy* (University of Chicago Press 1970).

[2] Idowu, S.O. & Capaldi, N. & Das Gypta, L.Z.A. (2013). Encyclopedia of Corporate Social Responsibility. *Springer Reference,* v.

[3] Ibid., v.

[4] Zhao, (2011). "Promoting more socially responsible corporations through UK company law after the 2008 financial crisis: the turning of the crisis compass" . International Company and Commercial Law Review 22(9): 275-284, 275; Roberts, P. C. "The American Idiocracy: The Crisis is Not Over", *Baltimore Chronicle,* February 3, 2010, at http://baltimorechronicle.com/2010/020410Roberts.shtml [accessed on January 23, 2014].

[5] Companies Act 2006.

Shareholder Value Principle (ESVP), embodied in Section 172, and the recent introduction of the new 414 sections, which obliges directors to develop a strategic report. The new Indian Companies Act 2013[6] will also be discussed, and the new compulsory CSR policy that the corporations must follow. In the conclusion, the author attempts to demonstrate that the support that CSR received, as well as the universally recognised benefits of it, shows that CSR is considered to be the future of corporate law, and not a fad whose time has come and gone.

2. THE 2008 FINANCIAL CRISIS

The 2008 crisis is to be remembered as one of the most shocking events in modern times. It led to the collapse of financial institutions, and to the bankruptcies of countries such as Pakistan and Iceland.[7] Some countries had to be bailed out on in order to avoid bankruptcy, Greece and Cyprus among others. Some factors that led to the crisis were "excessive risk-taking to boost financial firm stock prices", and the "substantial mortgage risks that remained within the banking system".[8] Furthermore, the absence of proper regulatory controls, accountability and transparency were also core factors that led to the 2008 crisis.[9] The victims of this misuse of corporate governance were the bank depositors, who remain in a vulnerable position.[10] Attempts, like the Financial Services of the United Kingdom Compensation Scheme, proved to be inadequate in the recent crisis.[11] Subsequently and desperately, in order to avoid panic and chaos in the banking system, governments attempted to protect the depositor's interests by bailing out the worst affected banks by nationalising, whether in part or in whole.[12] As a result of the crisis, the failed attempts, and the bailouts, depositors lost their confidence in the banks (and

[6] India, Companies Act 2013.
[7] Zhao (2011), 279.
[8] Bruner, C. M. (2010) "Corporate Governance: Reform in a Time of Crisis" 36 Journal of Corporate Law 309, 313.
[9] United Nations Global Compact. (2008) "The Global Economic Downturn: Why the UN Global Compact and .Corporate Sustainability Are Needed More Than Ever", *United Nation Global Compact Office*, New York available from http://www.unglobalcompact.org/newsandevents/news_archives/2008_10_17.html [accessed January 23, 2014].
[10] Zhao (2011), 279.
[11] Arora, A. (2011). "The Corporate Governance Failings in Financial Institutions and Directors' Legal Liability". 32 Company Lawyer 3, 7.
[12] Zhao J. (2011), 279.

generally in any other financial institution).[13] The crisis encouraged many researchers and organisations to re-evaluate various areas of law in order to find the causes that led to this situation.[14] It also pushed corporations to save themselves from insolvency, which effectively closed the door to CSR policies.[15] However, one reason for this direction is the lack of efficiency in implementing CSR policies.

Most of the CSR policies were made in a generic way and subsequently did not prove productive.[16] So how can corporations adhere to the CSR policies when they do not receive positive results? A correct incorporation of the CSR in the corporate governance of each company must be in some way connected with the business and strategy of each individual corporation. By applying this method, innovation and competitive advantage will improve substantially.[17] In the author's opinion, a correct use of CSR in the corporate governance of enterprises could help fix the problems of trust and confidence of stakeholders[18] and depositors that the financial crisis of 2008 created. The crisis showed that one of the most important assets in a corporation's arsenal is its intangible assets (human capital), and it can prove to be invaluable when they are in a harsh economic situation.[19] This article will examine the CSR and stakeholder theory, as these are both of vital importance in the corporate realm.

3. CORPORATE SOCIAL RESPONSIBILITY

Over time, the concept of CSR has become part of the business community, and has received support from myriads of scholars and nations.[20] Attempts to

---

[13] Financial Times, "Europe's Banking Confidence Crisis" Financial Times Editorial Comment, October 1, 2008 available from http://www.ft.com/cms/s/0/b8db7480-8fe4-11dd-9890-0000779fd18c.html#axzz2rDJR7p45 [accessed on January 23, 2014].

[14] Cabrelli, D. & Siems, M. (2013). "A Case-Based Approach to Comparative Company Law" at p1 in *Comparative Company Law: A Case-Based Approach.* Hart Publishing.

[15] Macalister, T. A Change in the climate: credit crunch makes the bottom-line the top issue. *The Guardian*, March 6 2008. Available from http://www.theguardian.com/business/2008/mar/06/greenbusiness.creditcrunch [accessed on the 13th of February 2014].

[16] Porter, M. E. & Kramer M. R. (2006), "Strategy & Society: The link between competitive advantage and Corporate Social Responsibility". *Harvard Business Review*, 1.

[17] Ibid., 2.

[18] Pedamon, C. (2010). "Corporate Social Responsibility: A New Approach to Promoting Integrity and Responsibility" (2010). 31 Company Lawyer 172, 172.

[19] Zhao (2011), 278.

[20] Porter and Kramer (2006), 1.

define CSR have continued for the last 30 years.[21] It does not always have the same meaning[22] or apply in the same way. For example, CSR policy for a corporation in China is to produce safe, high quality products, whereas in Germany, to provide secure employment, and in South Africa it is used for social development, such as health care and education.[23] The notion of CSR also overlaps with various concepts: sustainable business, corporate citizenship, environmental consideration, the triple bottom line, social and environmental accountability, business ethics, and corporate accountability.[24] CSR was defined as

> ...a concept whereby companies integrate social and environmental concerns in their business operations and in their interaction with their stakeholders on a voluntary basis";[25] or companies operate in an "...economically, socially, and environmentally sustainable manner, while recognizing the interests of its stakeholders, including investors, customers, employees, business partners, local communities, the environment, and society at large."[26]

This is supported by the fact that the broad definition of the concept has been adapted in different economic/social situations[27] and also works as a substitute for slow growing legislation, which tries to keep up with the lithe way in which corporations construe their business around the world.[28] Carroll, introduces his pyramid style diagram, which has been utilised by numerous theorists and empirical researchers.[29]

---

[21] Carroll A. B. (1991). "The Pyramid of Corporate Social Responsibility: Toward the Moral Management of Organizational Stakeholders, *Business Horizons*, July 1991, Vol 34(4): 39-48, see pages 39-40.

[22] Votaw, D. (1972). "Genius becomes rare: A comment on the doctrine of social responsibility". Pt. 1 California Management Review 15(2): 25-31, 25.

[23] Knox, S. (2007). "Corporate Social Responsibility and Business Decision Making" in *Spiritual Motivation: New Thinking for the Business and Management,* (eds. J. Ramsden, S. Aida, A. Kakabadse) Palgrave Macmillan, 147.

[24] Idowu and Capaldi, vii.

[25] European Commission. (2001) 'Prompting a European Framework for Corporate Social Responsibility', Green Paper and COM 366, Brussels. At page 6 (par. 2(20-26)) available from http://eur-lex.europa.eu/LexUriServ/site/en/com/2001/com2001_0366en01.pdf [accessed on 7th February 2013].

[26] Certified General Accountants Association of Canada. (2005). "Measuring up: A study on Corporate Sustainability Reporting in Canada," 20.

[27] Dunne, S. (2007) "What is Corporate Social Responsibility?" Ephemera 7(2): 372-380), 372.

[28] Idowu and Capaldi, v.

[29] Schwartz M. S. and Carroll, A. B. (2003). "Corporate Social Responsibility: A three-domain approach" Business Ethics Quarterly, Volume 13, Issue 4, 503-530, see page 504.

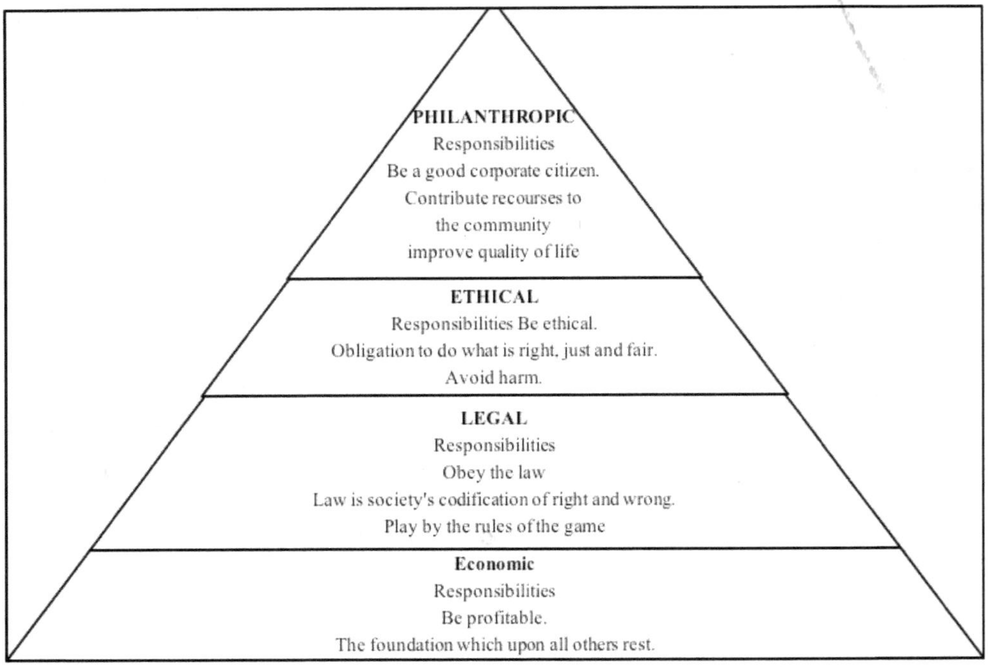

Figure 1: Carroll's Pyramid.[30]

The pyramid consists of four categories of economic, legal, ethical and philanthropic. Carroll proposes that these four layers compose CSR. The basis of the pyramid is the economic responsibility of the corporation to make profit. In order to do this, it must respect its legal responsibilities. The next two layers constitute CSR: ethical and philanthropic responsibilities. According to Carroll, there is a distinction between the ethical and the philanthropic, which is desirable but is the least important of the three.[31] Stakeholder theory is one of the most important enhancing mechanisms for CSR, as supported by Carroll: "There is a natural fit between the idea of corporate social responsibility and an organization's stakeholders".[32]

4. STAKEHOLDERS

The terms "stakeholder" and "stakeholder theory" overlap with CSR, and they play a big role in CSR. The main idea is that they link the financial interests of

[30] Carroll, 42.
[31] Ibid.
[32] Ibid.

a company with stakeholders' interests and provide methods of obtaining win-win situations. It is also suggested that when the director considers stakeholders' interests in their decision, the possibility of beneficial long-term progress is increased.[33] The term has been commonly accepted since Freeman's analysis in 1984,[34] and the concept was defined as the groups without which the corporation would not be able to exist.[35] Carroll termed stakeholders as

> …those groups or individuals with whom the organisation interacts or has interdependencies" and "any individual or group who can affect or is affected by the actions, decisions, policies practices or goals of the organisation.[36]

The definition is broad, and suggested that one way of increasing the consideration of the stakeholder groups is for directors to use a test of legitimacy (e.g. employees) and power (e.g. institutional investors)[37] in order to divide groups of stakeholders. Each corporation has different categories of stakeholders, depending on their course of business. Most frequently, stakeholders are employees, customers, creditors, local communities, the environment, government, or the public at large.[38] Clarkson defined the stakeholder theory as:

> The firm is a system of stakeholders operating within the larger system of the host society that provides the necessary legal and market infrastructure for the firm's activities. The purpose of the firm is to create wealth or value for its stakeholders by converting their stake into goods and services.[39]

The theory suggests that directors need to also consider the stakeholder's interests throughout the exercise of their duties. Figure 2 shows how the company interacts with various stakeholders. Their involvement in the

---

[33] Zhao, J. (2014) "The Curious case Stakeholder Theory: Calling a More Realistic Theory" International Trade and Business Law Review, 3.

[34] Ibid.

[35] Ibid., 5.

[36] Carroll, A. B. (1993). "Business society and stakeholders the business and society relationship" at page 10 and "Business Society and Stakeholders (The stakeholder approach to business society and ethics)" at page 84 in 2nd ed. *Business and Society: Ethics and Stakeholder Management*. Cincinnati: South-Western Publishing.

[37] Caroll, 43.

[38] Zhao, (2014), 2.

[39] Clarkson, M.B.E. (1994), "A Risk Based Model of Stakeholder Theory", The Centre for Corporate Social Performance & Ethics, University of Toronto.

corporation's performance is vital; without it the company would cease to exist.

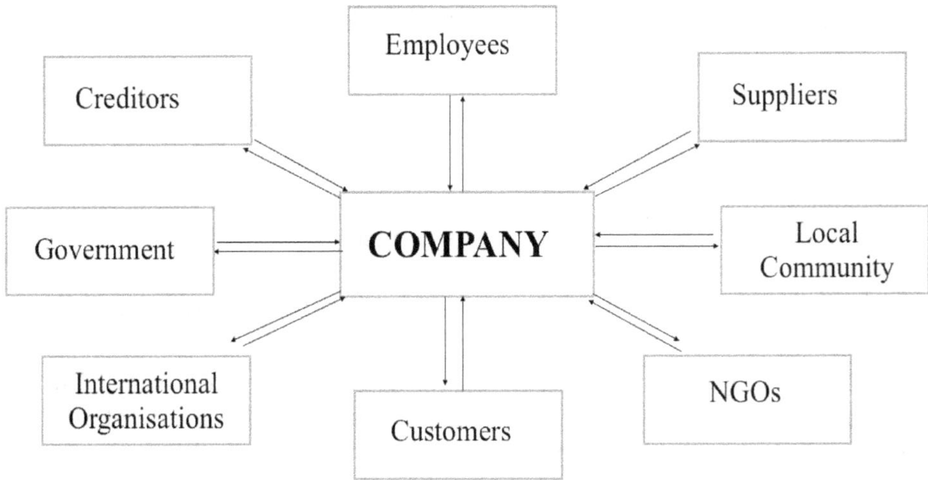

Figure 2: Corporation interaction with stakeholders[40]

5. BENEFITS OF CSR AND THE STAKEHOLDER THEORY

It would be, *de facto*, reasonable to consider the separate legal entity of a company as including various stakeholders that are bound together by their business activities.[41] Law determines the legal obligations of corporations, and directors, who act as agents of the corporations and act for the benefit of the "company as a whole". The ultimate goal for every corporation is to maximise total long-term market value,[42] and as Jensen correctly stated, "the change in the total long-term market value of the firms is the scorecard by which success is measured".[43] In the recently published Cox report, it has been shown that

[40] Donaldson T. & Preston L. E. (1995)."The Stakeholder Theory of the Corporation: Concept, Evidence, and Implications".20 Academy of Management Review 65 at 69.
[41] Zhao (2011), 277; Zhao, (2014), 42.
[42] Zhao (2011), 279.
[43] Jensen, M. C. (2001) 'Value Maximization, Stakeholder Theory, and the Corporate Objective Function' (2001) 14 Journal of Applied Corporate Finance 8, 246.

the short-termism is an established problem, and it was reiterated that long-term sustainability is the way forward.[44]

The consideration of stakeholders is important, as employees are the basis for increases in net profit, the creditors are the people responsible for providing the company with loan capital and suppliers, and they are a key factor for boosting competitiveness. This stakeholder approach combines the human capital created by employees, the equity capital of shareholders and the loan capital of creditors. These three factors then merge into an organic theory and assist the corporation in creating assets and subsequently becoming sustainable in the long run.[45] Lack of stakeholder consideration and a continuation short-termism will have consequences. Institutional investors will refrain from investing in these corporations, customers will not buy their products, the media will portray them in a negative light, and all of this in turn will have the consequence of hindering the financial growth of the company.[46] However, corporations can improve their competitiveness by considering various stakeholder groups.

Competitiveness is linked to sustainability and the maintenance of a company's reputation.[47] Reputation plays an important role in boosting competitiveness and at the same time setting foundations for sustainability. A way to raise the reputation of a company is by promoting CSR policies.[48] Campbell suggests that reputation has a "goodwill value," which can make the company more attractive to new consumers and investors by reflecting trust and confidence, and create a relationship of loyalty, which will be valuable in establishing a solid layer of stakeholders (employees, consumers, etc.). This layer can prove invaluable in situations of crisis and economic instability.[49] The media can also be a great way to advertise a firm's reputation, and the promotion of CSR attracts publicity and media attention.[50] The following diagram shows the consequences of organisational reputation and its interrelationship with the company.

---

[44] Cox, G. (2013). "Overcoming short-termism within British Business: the key to sustained economic growth". Labour Policy Review available from http://www.yourbritain.org.uk/uploads/editor/files/Overcoming_Short-termism.pdf. [accessed on 17th March 2014], 12-14, 26, 54.

[45] Zhao, (2014), 25.

[46] Buhmann, K. (2004). "Corporate Social Responsibility: What role for law? Some aspects of law and CSR". Emerald Group Publishing. Vol. 6 No. 2 (2006), 188-202, see page 190.

[47] Chen, C. H. (2011) "The major components of corporate social responsibility" *Journal of Global Responsibility* 2(1): 85-89, 88.

[48] Rindova, V.P., I.O. Williamson, A.P. Petkova, and J.M. (2005), "Being good or being known: an empirical examination of the dimensions, antecedents, and consequences of organizational reputation" Academy of Management Journal 48(6): 1033-49, 1033-1036.

[49] Campbell, M. C. (1999) "Perceptions of price unfairness: antecedents and consequences". Journal of Marketing Research 36(2): 187-99, 191.

[50] Rindova, Williamson, Petkova, Sever, (2005) 1037-1038.

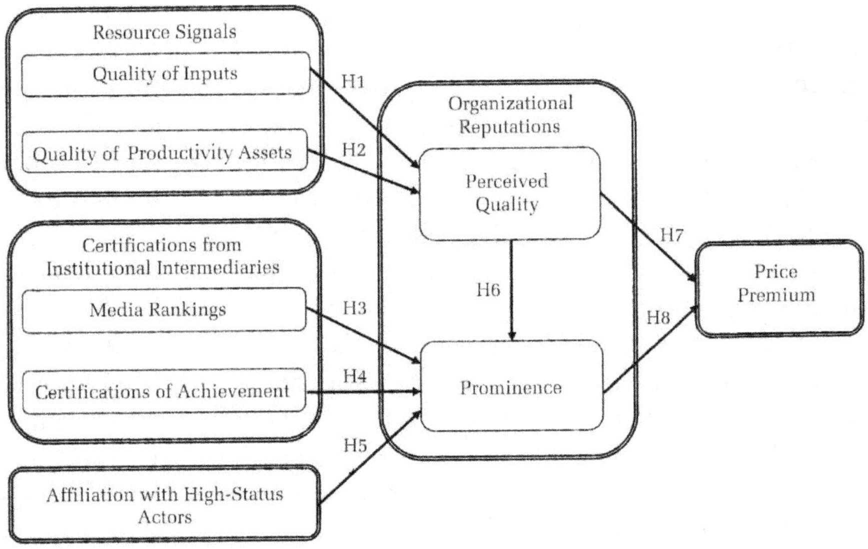

Figure 3: Antecedents and Consequences of Organisational reputation[51]

Pursuing the long-term interests of the company produces positive outcomes. Maintaining good relationships with stakeholders, when the directors respect and care about their interests, creates strong relationships within the company.[52] Disclosing the corporation's aims and goals enhances the establishment of a solid network of internal relationships, which boosts the potential of employees, who will perform at their best of their ability.[53] Building strong relationships with the local community and the Government also helps to make operations and development easier.[54] These well-established professional relationships, in conjunction with a strong reputation as well as the following policies inspired by the CSR, are key mechanisms which provide sustainability and create trust and confidence for the stakeholders group. Intangible assets and human capital are of vital importance for corporations, in order to promote the company as a whole.[55] The mistakes of the past are semantic, and it is the duty of all countries to legislate and avoid these issues in future.

Chen demonstrates the positive effects of CSR and correct corporate governance by distinguishing the business operation of two corporations' giants in Taiwan: Procomp and TSMC. The former was involved in financial

[51] Ibid.
[52] Zhao (2011), 277.
[53] Zhao, (2014), 38.
[54] Zhao (2011), 278.
[55] Ibid.

scandals, which led to the collapse of the company after a failure of corporate governance, lack of transparency, and less accountability (i.e. ethically).[56] On the other hand, TSMC has always acted with honesty, integrity and transparency; paying important consideration to long-term interests.[57] It has received various awards that recognise its achievements, and has become a role model for its excellent corporate governance, and above all, its dedication to CSR has made the TSMC one of the world's leading corporations. A reason for the Procomp and Enron's problems was the result of excessive risk taking and short-termism, which led to scandals and abuse of human capital. CSR and the stakeholder theory, among other overlapping conceptual foundations, are founded on ethical standards. This approach has been supported worldwide, not just by academia, but also by countries and organisations.

6. CSR IN THE MODERN WORLD

Researchers have found that the best companies around the world base their effective management on social and environmental policies.[58] There are many organisations promoting CSR that provide certifications and media publications for companies. One of them is a U.S based organisation, with over 900 member companies worldwide (B corporation), which aims to promote companies which are not only in the pursuit of becoming the best in the world, but also the best for the world.[59] The organisation attracts corporations by giving them a certification of membership. It promotes pure principles of CSR and embraces a more socio-environmental policy towards stakeholders. Another example is the Cockburn Report,[60] which was welcomed by the Department of Innovation and Skills (DTI). The report provides extensive guidance for experienced and inexperienced companies regarding CSR. It also provides an excellent explanation of the commercial benefits and positive impacts of considering various stakeholders, and other key areas of a socially responsible corporate company. Moreover, in the UK, almost eighty per cent of the pension scheme members are now operating in a

---

[56] Chen (2011), 86.

[57] Ibid.

[58] Snider, J., Hill R. and Martin D. (2003), "Corporate social responsibility in the 20th century: a view from the world's most successful firms" Journal of Business Ethics 48: 175-87, 180-181.

[59] www.bcorporation.net, available information about the company at http://www.bcorporation.net/what-are-b-corps [accessed 11th February 2014] .

[60] Cockburn Report. (2000). "Winning with integrity". Available from http://www.orendaconnections.com/Winning-with-integrity-Summary.pdf [accessed on 16th of March 2014] .

social investment policy.[61] The UK also passed the Companies Act 2006, in which the Company Law Review Steering Group's (CLRSG) recommendation of the enlightened shareholder value (ESVP) which will be discussed below, was incorporated. There was also a recent amendment, making the disclosure of strategic report compulsory.

7. ESVP AND STRATEGIC REPORT

The stakeholder theory is embraced in many continental European countries such as France and Germany, but also further afield, in Japan. However, the situation is not the same for Anglo-American corporations. Anglo-American corporate law has always been traditionally shareholder-centric, and some academics suggest that the UK has a model even more shareholder-oriented than the U.S.[62] Major legislative reforms in 2006 introduced a new corporate orientation for the first time in the UK. The Companies Act introduced section 172, which is a shift from the traditional *status quo* of corporate English law to a more socially responsible sphere. Section 172 incorporates 'enlightened shareholder value'[63] (ESVP). This was developed by the CLRSG in June 2001,[64] and is embodied in Section 172. The question of to whom a director owes a duty has been debated since the 1930s, commonly known as the Berle-Dodd debate,[65] and Section 172 answers that question. There are 3 keywords in the section; "in good faith", "the success of the company" and "have regard".[66]

The first duty is quite broad, and the director has discretion here. It is occasionally interpreted as a fiduciary duty arising from the agency relationship between the director and the corporation. Nevertheless, as Keay argues, the directors make their position "virtually unassailable" by claiming that they acted in good faith.[67] Secondly, the success of the company gives legitimacy to the directors, who have a broad level of discretion as to what to acknowledge when they make their decisions. In the Grand Chamber debate, Lord Goldsmith described the success of the company as what the corporation

---

[61] Zhao (2014), 30.

[62] Bruner (2010), 310.

[63] Copp, S. F. (2009). "Corporate Social Responsibility and the Companies Act 2006" . Economic Affairs 29(4): 16-21, 16.

[64] Company Law Review Steering Group (2000) Modern Company Law for a Competitive Economy: Developing the Framework, London: Department of Trade and Industry ('DTF, 2000') .

[65] Sheikh, S. (1996). "Are Corporate manager Trustees?" in 1st ed. *Corporate Social Responsibilities: Law & Practice*, Cavendish, 153-157.

[66] Companies Act 2006, s172.

[67] Keay, A. (2007) "Section 172(1) of the Companies Act 2006: An Interpretation and Assessment" . The Company Lawyer 29(4) 4: 106–110, 108.

goal is. For example, a commercial corporation should strive for a long-term increase.[68] Lastly, the words "have regard" are seen for the first time in UK history, and seem to give authority to the directors to consider not just the shareholders of the company but also the stakeholders.[69] In the author's opinion, the introduction of ESVP (which is purely inspired by CSR and stakeholder theory) to Anglo-American corporations, is considered to be a big step in showing that CSR is still on the political agenda and consequently on the corporation's agenda. Recently there was another regulatory amendment by the UK, which makes the disclosure of information compulsory.

The duty was imposed by the recent Companies Act 2006 (Strategic Report and Directors' Report) Regulations 2013,[70] which has been approved and took effect on the 1st of October 2013. Section 414 is particularly important because it introduces a new duty to the directors of the company to prepare a strategic report for each year.[71] The purpose of this strategic report is to disclose company information to members regarding efficiency, along with the director's performance, under Section 172.[72] Section 414C states that the report must include the central financial thesis, principal risks and uncertainties facing the company. It must also incorporate an analysis of key performance indicators and, most importantly, it must include the main factors which are likely to affect the company's development, performance, and business in the future. The regulations also set three examples of future factors which may affect the company. These are: environmental matters, company's employees, community and human rights issues.[73] The duty to disclose information is beneficial for corporations. The directors are obliged to present such a report, which will in fact be an assessment of their own work ethic, according to Section 172. Another major legislative reform is the new Companies Act in India, which came with a surprising provision.

8. INDIA COMPANIES ACT 2013

The Parliament of India passed the Companies Act 2013, replacing the previous 56-year-old Act. The Indian economy was based on a socialist model

---

[68] (Hansard (HL) 6 February 2006, cols 255- 256.

[69] Copp (2009), 19.

[70] Statutory Instruments; The Companies Act 2006 (Strategic Report) Regulations 2013. No. 1970.

[71] Ibid., s414A.

[72] Ibid., s414C.

[73] Ibid., s414C, (1)-(14).

and corporate activities were minimal.[74] However, with India becoming an economic power in the 21st century, the law was not capable of regulating such rapid corporate development. This resulted in huge corporate scandals, and a legal framework with high standards was needed.[75] The author is concerned with Section 135 of the Act, which states that under some financial criteria, a company must have a Corporate Social Responsibility Committee board, consisting of three or more directors.[76] The committee must formulate and recommend CSR Policies (which under Schedule IV is described to include a broad category of stakeholders connected with the corporation), including help towards society and the Government. These include: poverty reduction, education, health, environmental sustainability, gender equality, and the development of vocational skills.[77] The crux of the Act is Section 135 (5), which states that corporations are obliged to spend at least two per cent of their average net profits towards the proposed CSR policy, and in case the company fails to do so, the board must disclose the reasons why.[78] This section has a huge impact on modern company law, as India is the first to mandate the CSR. The section embodies stakeholder theory, CSR, as well as strong elements of corporate citizenship. The author acknowledges the theory behind this "corporate citizen duty", which is that the corporation must offer something back to society, community, government, etc., and then, by using the domestic legal system and corporate field, increase the power and the capital of the corporation. Additionally, this is considered to be a new way of interpreting the CSR in countries with very levels of low societal development.

9. CONCLUSION

The financial crisis of 2008 is a wake up call for countries to revise their corporate governance regulation for the future. Organisations (UN) and certain jurisdictions are already taking action regarding the lack of corporate governance. Transparency, accountability, excessive risk and short-term profits are all problems that the business community must ultimately solve. The Cox report highlighted that long-term sustainability is considered to be the new way forward, and the best way to accomplish this is through the incorporation of CSR and stakeholder policies in a company's corporate

---

[74]Ramaswamy, S. (2014). "Companies Act 2013: A critical analysis of the proposed new company law in India" International Company and Commercial Law Review 25(1): 31-35, 31.

[75] Ibid., 31.

[76] India, Companies Act 2013.

[77] Ibid., section 135(3)(a)–(c).

[78] Ibid., section 135(5).

structure. These concepts were not implemented correctly pre-2008 and were not beneficial to companies: this was the main reason why corporations seemed to erase CSR from their daily agenda. As the evidence suggests, following policies based on CSR and stakeholder theory help promoting a corporation's competitiveness, which in turn leads to long-term sustainability. The consideration of employees also provides various benefits, like creating solid interrelationships within the company and thereby increasing net profits. Without a doubt, after the 2008 crisis, intangible assets are one of the most important assets that a corporation can acquire. Moreover, the stakeholder approach of "organic theory" is an excellent example, which demonstrates how corporations can grow assets and substantial long-term profits. These policies have been supported by several organisations and have been promoted by the European Union, United Nations and other countries. The ESVP and Section 414 are a brief example of where the UK, for the first time, has given legitimacy to directors to look outside the box and consider the company as a whole. Also, the requirement of a strategic report is another great attempt towards creating more socially responsible corporate companies. The duty to disclose information is considered to be the core of CSR and stakeholder theory, and is envisaged in section 414. Furthermore, the introduction of the Indian Act is considered to have a huge impact on the country as a whole, since India is the first country to mandate CSR, which in the author's opinion gives the assumption that a company has duties as a corporate citizen. The evidence also suggests that there is plenty of acknowledgment of what the problematic factors of the crisis are, and that people are more skeptical as to how the corporation works; that is why CSR must be strictly implemented. Corporations and countries, which want competitive corporate law and to compete with other legal systems (like Delaware) and economies around the world, are aware of this, and that is why one can see so much orientation towards CSR and stakeholders. These reforms and the orientation towards CSR proves this is not merely a fad whose time has come and gone, but indeed a new layer of regulation that is trying to blend with the previous corporate legal system. The layer will serve as a safeguard not just for providing indirect regulation but also protecting from abuse of corporate ethics, and prevent future economic instability such as increased government debt and inflation. The future of CSR is uncertain, although as evidence suggests, it is being established in corporate law for good, and, as Zhao and Freeman support, the idea must disappear in a way that its principles emerge in corporate law in the future.[79]

---

[79] Zhao, J., *Corporate Social Responsibility in Contemporary China*. Cheltenham : Edward Elgar Publishing (2014), 261-262.

The Illusion of Choice—Have Enforced Caesarean Cases Introduced a New Class of Incompetent Adults?

Mabel Wei[†]

In Norfolk and Norwich Healthcare NHS Trust v W[1], *Justice Johnson found a mother incompetent to refuse a caesarean section despite not suffering from any mental disability because, as a result of "acute emotional stress and physical pain in the ordinary course of labour"*[2]*, he believed that she was not able to weigh up the information presented to her. On that very same day, Johnson J similarly decided in* Rochdale Healthcare NHS Trust v C[3] *that the mother was not capable of weighing the information given to her because she "was in the throes of labour with all that is involved in terms of pain and emotional stress"*[4]*. Besides suggesting that the state of labour has a bearing on finding the patient incapable, Johnson J went further to assess the content of the patient's refusal—that one who was able "to accept the inevitability of her own death" was evidence of someone who was incapable of weighing up the information, therefore her refusal of a caesarean section that could potentially save her life would be invalid.*[5] *These two cases illustrate the creation of a catch-22 situation, whereby if a competent mother exercises her discretion to refuse medical intervention, the psychiatrist and judge would consider the mother incompetent by virtue of that very decision. The corollary is that "women in labour may only have the capacity to withhold consent as long as they do not".*[6] *Such an illusion of autonomy*

† Final Year LLB Candidate, University of Leicester School of Law.

1 [1997] 1 FCR 269.

2 Ibid., 272.

3 [1997] 1 FCR 274.

4 Ibid., 275.

5 Ibid.

6 Ceri Widdett & Michael Thomson, "Justifying Treatment and Other Stories" [1997] 5 FLS 77, 86.

demonstrates how pregnant women have implicitly been newly classed as incompetent adults.

Keywords: Enforced caesarean section, patient autonomy, right to life, incompetent adult, consent, Mental Capacity Act 2005

1. Introduction

Lord Donaldson, Master of the Rolls, so accurately prognosticated in *Re T*[7] that should the situation arise where a mother's refusal to undergo a caesarean section operation would endanger the life of a viable foetus, "the courts [would] be faced with a novel problem of considerable legal and ethical complexity".[8] Such a situation indeed arose two months later,[9] unfolding a cascade of similar caesarean cases that generated passionate discourse in the judiciary and among academics alike. Much of the discourse centered around the competence of pregnant women, their rights, and the hospital's enforceability of caesarean sections where refusal would be a detriment to either the mother or foetus, or both. This article will first introduce the common law relating to consent and whether it can be reconciled with the caesarean cases. Subsequently, it will explore whether the caesarean cases have indeed introduced a new class of incompetent adults, who have lost the right to make their own decisions during pregnancy to paramount medical interests. This article precludes discussion of caesarean cases in jurisdictions other than the United Kingdom (UK).

2. 'Consent' under Common Law

As alluded to, enforced caesarean cases have been controversial, particularly concerning the validity of a mother's refusal to undergo a caesarean section operation, when such a refusal would endanger her own life, her foetus' chance of survival, or both. For a consent or refusal to be valid, firstly, the patient making it has to have capacity. The functional test for capacity as set out in *Re C*[10] (a non-caesarean case) was reiterated in *Re MB* by Lady Butler-Sloss: "a person lacked capacity if… [she were] unable to comprehend and

---

[7] *(Adult: Refusal of Treatment)* [1992] 3 WLR 782.
[8] Ibid., 8.
[9] In the case of *Re S (Adult: Refusal of Treatment)* [1992] 4 All ER 671.
[10] *(Adult: Refusal of Treatment)* [1994] 2 FCR 151, 153.

retain… [and] use the information and weigh it in the balance."[11] As such, *Re MB* brought the common law governing consent to the fore of enforced caesarean cases—unless a mother could not comprehend, retain and use that information to weigh it in the balance, she would be considered to have the capacity to refuse any medical intervention, including a caesarean section operation. This test for capacity is now codified in Section 3(1) of the Mental Capacity Act (MCA) 2005. Furthermore, such a refusal would be valid even if it were based on "rational or irrational reasons or… no reasons at all".[12] In line with the functional test set out in *Re C*, *Re MB* confirms that the content of and reasons behind the refusal would not matter, so long as the mother is functional or competent enough to make that decision to refuse.

Secondly, a valid consent or refusal has to be an informed one. *Wyatt v Curtis*[13], in support of Lord Bridge's test in *Sidaway*[14], confirms that an informed consent comprises information that a reasonable patient would want to be informed of by a reasonable doctor.[15] As regards to caesarean cases, it has generally not been contentious whether or not decisions were informed. Thirdly, only a voluntary refusal or consent would be valid.[16] Therefore, the validity of consent within caesarean cases is consistent with the common law rules relating to consent. However, this reconciliation does little to address the complexities that plague the caesarean cases, one of which is whether a new class of incompetent adults has emerged from such cases.

3. A NEW CLASS OF INCOMPETENT ADULTS?

Re S[17] pioneers the enforced caesarean situation in the legal context, where an emergency declaration was sought by the hospital to enforce a caesarean section, which the mother refused on religious grounds. Sir Stephen Brown P granted the declaration, overriding the mother's autonomy to refuse while placing emphasis on the "life of the unborn child".[18] Despite the failure to find that the mother had lacked capacity to refuse the operation, Lord Justice Thorpe boldly opined that if put in a similar position at that time, he and the judges of the Family Division would have had arrived at the same decision.[19]

---

[11] *(An Adult: Medical Treatment)* [1997] 2 FCR 541.
[12] Ibid.
[13] [2003] EWCA Civ 1779.
[14] *Sidaway v Bethlem Royal Hospital Governors* [1985] 1 All ER 643.
[15] *Wyatt*, para 16.
[16] *Re T.*
[17] *Re S.*
[18] Ibid., 672.
[19] Mathew Alexander Thorpe, "Consent for Caesarean Section: Part 1 Development of the Law" [2000] Catholic Medical Quarterly.

Besides being clearly contrary to the laws of capacity and consent as outlined above, religious considerations are "neither rational nor irrational; they are nonrational and are therefore, amendable neither to verification or falsification".[20] In other words, a decision based on religious grounds does not render it irrational and certainly does not and cannot suggest or affirm a patient's incapacity. The decision in *Re S* has been described as "inappropriate"[21] and "worrying"[22]; this is rightly so because it encourages a plethora of problems, such as the erosion of the fundamental human right to bodily integrity and the disintegration of effective doctor-patient communication, since patients can no longer trust that doctors have their interests at heart[23]. Fortunately, the common law governing enforced caesareans has since at least attempted to shift away from the unsound stance in *Re S.*

Apart from the above-mentioned *Re MB,* the Court of Appeal in *R v Collins, ex parte S*[24] also reaffirmed the validity of a competent mother's refusal of medical intervention, irrespective of the consequences to both herself and the foetus. Although the judge at first instance, Mrs. Justice Hogg, authorized the nonconsensual treatment, that decision was overruled by the Court of Appeal for a number of reasons.[25] Most pertinently, Hogg J made no particular reference to the competence of Ms. S in her decision to authorize the declaration. The Court of Appeal eventually found Ms. S to be competent despite the declaration, since she was able to understand, retain, believe and weigh up the information to reach a decision.[26] This was also supported by the fact that Ms. S' psychiatrist had found her to have the capacity to consent to or refuse medical treatment. The Court of Appeal plainly held that the hospital must accept a competent patient's decision. While *Re MB* and *ex parte S* seem to bend in favour of the view that the caesarean cases do not make pregnant women a new class of incompetent adults, some academics have observed that judges and medical professionals have conversely used pregnancy as a mark

---

<http://www.cmq.org.uk/CMQ/2000/consent_for_caesarean_1.htm> accessed 31 December 2014, p 5.

[20] Heather Cahill, "An Orwellian Scenario: Court Ordered Caesarean Section and Women's Autonomy" [1999] 6 *Nursing Ethics* 494, 496.

[21] Royal College of Obstetricians and Gynaecologists, *A Consideration of the Law and Ethics in Relation to Court-Authorized Obstetric Interventions* (London, 1994) 5.12.

[22] Kristina Stern, "Court-Ordered Caesarian Sections: In Whose Interests?" [1993] 56 MLR 238, 243.

[23] Aurora Plomer, "Judicially Enforced Caesareans and the Sanctity of Life" [1997] 26 Anglo-American Law Review 235.

[24] [1998] 3 All ER 673.

[25] *Cahill*, 4.

[26] *Ex parte S*, 681.

of psychiatric illness to cast doubt on a mother's capacity to consent or refuse.[27]

Such an instance occurred in *Norfolk and Norwich Healthcare NHS Trust v W*[28], where Justice Johnson found a mother to be incompetent despite not suffering from any mental disability because, as a result of "acute emotional stress and physical pain in the ordinary course of labour"[29], he believed that she was not able to weigh up the information presented to her. On that very same day, Johnson J similarly decided in *Rochdale Healthcare NHS Trust v C*[30] that the mother was not capable of weighing the information given to her because she "was in the throes of labour with all that is involved in terms of pain and emotional stress"[31]. Besides suggesting that the state of labour has a bearing on finding the patient incapable, Johnson J went further to assess the content of the patient's refusal—that one who was able "to accept the inevitability of her own death" was evidence of someone who was incapable of weighing up the information, therefore her refusal would be invalid.[32] These two cases illustrate the creation of a catch-22 situation, whereby if a competent mother exercises her discretion to refuse medical intervention, the psychiatrist and judge would consider the mother incompetent by virtue of that very decision. The corollary is that "women in labour may only have the capacity to withhold consent as long as they do not".[33] As such, these two caesarean cases seem to have made pregnant women a new class of incompetent adults. Granted, the decisions in *Re MB* and *ex parte S* have since explicitly afforded competent pregnant mothers the capacity to make a valid refusal, regardless of the content or reasons behind it, however, those decisions did not address the catch-22 situation that was canvassed by *Norfolk* and *Rochdale*.

The paternalistic practice underlying *Norfolk* and *Rochdale* finds its root in implicit assumptions of incompetence[34]; that a mother's refusal to undergo a beneficial caesarean section operation need not be respected because it is so detrimental that it must carry with it an element of incompetence[35]. The judiciary, which demonstrably prefers erring on the side of life, is able to use

---

[27] Ceri Widdett & Michael Thomson, "Justifying Treatment and Other Stories" [1997] 5 FLS 77; Lieve Gies, "Contesting the Rule of Emotions? The Press and Enforced Caesareans" [2000] 9 SLS 515, p 524; Sabine Michalowski, "Court-Authorised Caesarean Sections – The End of a Trend" [1999] 62 Modern Law Review 115.

[28] [1997] 1 FCR 269.

[29] Ibid., 272.

[30] [1997] 1 FCR 274.

[31] Ibid., 275.

[32] Ibid.

[33] Widdett, 86.

[34] Cahill, 498.

[35] John Harris, *The Value of Life: An Introduction to Medical Ethics* (first published 1985, Routledge 1990), 198.

the discretion afforded by common law when determining competence to accommodate such assumptions, thus sneaking paternalism through this "back-door".[36] In *ex parte S*, Lord Donaldson MR quoted *Re T*, drawing attention to the importance of the level of risk that a refusal would expose the mother or foetus to, when deciding on the issue of competence.[37] MacLean rightly pointed out that being concerned with such a "risk-related standard of competence" would afford the judiciary discretion to "shift the goal posts and demand an unreachable level of competence in order to find the woman incompetent and so protect the foetus".[38] Furthermore, it would be easy for a judge to explicitly affirm the refusals of all competent mothers, when he knows that he could simply employ the unique facts of the case before him to deem that one mother incompetent and so authorize the enforced caesarean—in *Re MB*, the mother was deemed incompetent due to her needle phobia. These caesarean cases and their corresponding analyses seem to suggest that the pathway for an illusion of autonomy has been paved, built on the notion that pregnant mothers have become a new class of incompetent adults.

In addition, it has been observed that if a mother declared an intention to refuse a caesarean section operation as part of her birth plan, she might be liable to detention under section 2 of the Mental Health Act 1983, upon the recommendation of two registered medical practitioners, for the interests of her own health or safety.[39] A birth plan is a non-legally binding document that healthcare professionals can refer to when a pregnant mother is in labour; it is intended to empower the pregnant mother by allowing her to declare her choices as regards to her labour process and its aftermath.[40] However, what is the point of ascertaining a mother's needs and wishes through birth plans if they would not be acceded to should they not align with the hospital's agenda? Clearly, hospitals continue to parent mothers' decisions. As such, the effectiveness of birth plans with developing the law regarding caesarean cases is questionable as to whether it is a step towards or away from empowering mothers. Thus far, it seems that the caesarean cases have implicitly made possibly competent women into a new class of incompetent adults, all the while explicitly declaring that a competent pregnant mother's refusal would be valid. Nevertheless, no matter how much inclination judges have towards

---

[36] Alasdair MacLean, "Caesarean Sections, Competence and the Illusion of Autonomy" [1999] 1 *WebJCLI*.

[37] *Ex parte S*.

[38] Maclean.

[39] Caroline Wells, "On the Outside Looking In: Perspectives on Enforced Caesareans". In: Sally Sheldon & Michael Thomson, *Feminist Perspectives on Health Care Law* (Cavendish 1998), 237-255.

[40] National Health Service, 'How To Make a Birth Plan' (5 February 2015) <http://www.nhs.uk/Conditions/pregnancy-and-baby/pages/how-to-make-birth-plan.aspx#close> accessed 9 October 2015.

deeming a pregnant mother incompetent, statute places restrictions on how far they can assume incapacity—or at least that was what the MCA 2005 intended to do.

4. CONTRIBUTION BY THE MCA 2005

In *Re AA*[41], Justice Mostyn authorized a declaration for a lawful enforced caesarean section. Despite explicitly acknowledging that his decision is to be "made squarely within the four corners of the [MCA] 2005",[42] there is little in his judgment that evidence his deference to the Act. Mostyn J classed AA as lacking capacity under section 2(1) MCA 2005 by virtue of her being detained under the Mental Health Act (MHA) 1983.[43] Although AA's inability to make decisions was conceded by her lawyer, in deciding what were in AA's best interests under section 4 MCA 2005, Mostyn J did not engage in any of AA's interests besides those of medical nature; there was no attempt to engage AA to make her own decisions or consult her kin's views; authorization of the caesarean section operation was definitely not the least restrictive alternative because Mostyn J could have instead ordered AA's restraint to obtain the foetus' heartbeat; the fact that AA could have at some point regained capacity was not at all considered. All these overlooked factors were for the purpose of an invasive operation that would avoid a mere 1% risk to AA's health. It is clear from this case that MCA 2005 had not benefited AA in any way, much less placed restrictions on allowing pregnant mothers to be classed as incompetent adults.

The case of *Great Western Hospitals NHS Foundation Trust v AA and others*[44] is slightly more heartening. Bearing in mind that the patient in *Re AA* was thirty-nine weeks pregnant and the patient in this case was thirty-eight weeks pregnant—only one week earlier, in this case, much greater effort was put in and communication with relevant persons transpired to determine the patient's capacity under section 3 MCA 2005 and to ascertain what were in the patient's best interests under section 4 MCA 2005. Justice Hayden authorized the enforced caesarean after giving due consideration to the patient's earlier wishes of wanting a healthy baby, as well as her partner and father's support of the medical professionals' recommendations,[45] and also based on the fact that psychiatric assessments conducted by two psychiatrists both concluded on the patient's incapacity[46]. However, this case only

[41] [2012] EWHC 4378.
[42] Ibid., para 1.
[43] Ibid., para 2.
[44] [2014] EWHC 132.
[45] Ibid., para 16-17.
[46] Ibid., para 19-20.

demonstrates that under the MCA 2005, judges now consider more factors when deciding what is in the patient's best interests after deeming them incompetent. The MCA 2005 makes it no more difficult than common law to class pregnant mothers as incompetent.

NHS Trust and others v FG[47] also seems to resonate with the assertion that the contributions made by the MCA 2005 to caesarean cases are limited. In *FG*, instead of plainly applying the MCA 2005, Justice Keehan set out detailed procedural and substantive guidance relating to urgent applications seeking declarations for lawful medical treatment.[48] His guidelines prove to be more instructive—and perhaps more restrictive—than existing law on the circumstances in which such applications should be made when a pregnant woman who is diagnosed with a psychiatric illness is involved. For example, the applicant needs to have a "great degree of confidence" that active restraint of the pregnant woman would be required.[49] From the above-mentioned recent cases, it can be seen that the MCA 2005 has hardly contributed to the common law regarding caesarean cases. Additionally, while it is notable that the guidelines in *FG* might actually be a step against assuming pregnant women as incompetent adults, compliance with them remains to be seen. Despite all that has been said and done, pregnant mothers have yet to succeed escaping from this illusion of autonomy, thus the stance that the caesarean cases have implicitly made pregnant women into a new class of incompetent adults still persists.

5. THE BALANCING ACT

A concept of utmost centrality to the issue of a pregnant woman's capacity to consent or refuse is the fundamental principle of autonomy. It would be undoubtedly inaccurate to simply suggest that patients have lost the right to make their own decisions during pregnancy, because surely they would be able to make uncomplicated decisions such as whether or not they want to watch television. This essay is concerned only with the right to make decisions regarding invasive medical treatments, which has been the contentious issue of the caesarean cases.

The principle of adult autonomy has been established by common law and enshrined in Article 8 of the European Convention on Human Rights (ECHR), the right to respect for private life, which includes self-determination of one's own mortality and acceptance of medical treatments. Moreover, as Lord Donaldson MR provided in *Re T*, this "right of choice…exists

---

[47] [2014] EWCOP 30.
[48] Ibid., para 72-130 and Annex.
[49] Ibid., para 115.

notwithstanding that the reasons for making the choice are rational, irrational, unknown or even non-existent".[50] However, in the same judgment, he also suggested that breaching such a right might be qualified in enforced caesarean cases, where the decision to refuse the caesarean section operation would "lead to the death of a viable foetus".[51] This is in line with Mill's harm principle, which suggests that only benefit to a third party can justify overriding one's autonomy.[52] As such, in enforced caesarean cases, judges often find themselves having to weigh the principle of autonomy against the sanctity of life, to balance the mother's right to self-determination and the foetus' right to life.

However, the arguments against a foetus' right to life have been proposed and accepted on numerous occasions. In *Paton v United Kingdom*[53], it was held that Article 2 of the ECHR, the right to life, would not apply to a foetus and that the life of the mother would supersede that of the foetus. *Re F*[54] confirmed the decision in *Paton* that an unborn child has no legal rights or existence. *Ex parte S* squarely places these decisions in the context of caesarean cases, holding that "an unborn child is not a separate person from its mother. Its need for medical assistance does not prevail over her rights. She is entitled not to be forced to submit to an invasion of her body against her will, whether her own life or that of her unborn child depends on it. Her right is not reduced or diminished merely because her decision to exercise it may appear morally repugnant… Unless lawfully justified this constituted an infringement of the mother's autonomy… [P]erceived needs of the fetus did not provide the necessary justification."[55] As such, on the scales, the balance seems to tip in favour of the adult mothers' right to make their own decisions when weighed against the foetus' medical interests. Furthermore, forcing a mother to make decisions for the benefit of her foetus could be opening the gateway to other invasive fetal therapies.[56]

However, Draper warns against taking such an approach in enforced caesarean cases because by focusing on resolving conflicting rights between the mother's autonomy and foetus' right to life, one neglects the importance of the reasons behind the mother's reluctance to consent.[57] A mother could very well be refusing treatment because she feels that it is in the best interests

[50] *Re T*, n 7.
[51] Ibid.
[52] John Stuart Mill, *On Liberty* (Oxford, Oxford University Press, 1859).
[53] [1980] 3 EHRR 408.
[54] *(in utero)* [1998] Fam 122.
[55] *Ex parte S*, 692.
[56] Heather Draper, "Women, Forced Caesareans and Antenatal Responsibilities" [1996] 22 JME 327, 328.
[57] Ibid.

of her foetus,[58] or because she distrusts the medical advice she received", like in *Re S*, where the facts suggest that there was likely a communication breakdown between S and her caregivers.[59] Draper suggests that a better approach would be for judges to focus on "how much one person can reasonably be expected to sacrifice in order to save the life of another, especially when the chances of actually succeeding are remote".[60] However, in my view, Draper's approach is not in any way less complex an ethical conundrum than the balancing of rights and more pertinently, it would afford judges an unbelievably broad range of discretion to impose their paternalistic standards on pregnant women, such as requiring them to sacrifice their right to refuse life-saving treatment in most circumstances. Judges would also reign free to arbitrarily determine which sorts of reasons provided by mothers justify their refusal to medical intervention and which do not. Deviating the focus of the discussion on enforced caesareans from balancing rights to considering reasons for refusal and reasonable expectations might actually backfire and create much inconsistency, undermining the predictability of the law. Regardless, the principle of autonomy currently stands rather firmly against the foetus' right to life, thus affording mothers the right to make their own decisions during pregnancy. However, it is difficult to ignore the fact that in every caesarean case discussed thus far, the applications for enforced caesarean operations have been granted. This is not least because of the paternalistic practices adopted by judges, as expounded on above.

While I do not agree, I am able to empathize with judges who incline towards such paternalistic approaches. With such far-reaching and serious consequences flowing from their decisions, it is understandable that judges, facing the time constraints of emergency applications that are common to the enforced caesarean cases, prefer erring on the side of life by giving greater weightage to medical interests rather than patient autonomy.[61] These decisions find themselves attuning to utilitarian[62] motives, where the life of the foetus and public interest is protected, at the expense of the mother being deemed incompetent and hence robbed of her autonomy. Utilitarianism treats mothers as mere means to an end—that end being overall happiness or health—therefore deprivation of their rights to achieve that end would be justified. In my view, a better approach lies in deontology, whereby Scheffler put forward a deontological rights-based theory that treats mothers as ends in themselves and therefore should not be deprived of their autonomy.[63] This perspective is

---

[58] See *In Re AC* (1987) 533 A.2d 611.

[59] Cahill, 501.

[60] Draper, 329.

[61] *Re E* [2012] EWHC 1639, para 140.

[62] Jeremy Bentham, *A Fragment on Government* (London 1776), Preface.

[63] Samuel Scheffler, *The Rejection of Consequentialism* (Oxford: Oxford University Press, 1982).

attractive because affording mothers their autonomy would encourage maternal altruism and effective doctor-patient relationships that culminate in overall medical benefit.[64] In stark contrast, allowing utilitarianism to champion a healthcare system would be to permit John Harris' projection of a perfectly utilitarian organ lottery, whereby only the random organ donor suffers for the many who would benefit from his organs, thereby increasing overall health.[65] Such a barbaric possibility finds no place in society today. Fortunately, one can be consoled by the fact that deontological perspectives underlie the principles explicit in *ex parte S*—that a competent mother's right to self-determination must be respected, and both in *Re C* and *Re MB*—that a competent person possesses the autonomy to make a valid informed consent or refusal, which once again reinforces that the caesarean cases do reconcile with the common law rules relating to consent.

6. Conclusion

It has been made explicit by decisions of the above-mentioned caesarean cases that as long as the conditions stated in *Re MB* for establishing capacity are met, "pregnancy does not diminish [that] competent adult patient's right to refuse unwanted medical intervention"[66]; this is consistent with the common law governing consent as set out in *Re C*. However, since the relationship between competence and the right to self-determination is inextricably linked, whether pregnant women would be able to exercise rights that have been conferred to them by common law would depend on how well they fare against paternalistic assumptions of their incompetence. Although it has been well over a decade since *Norfolk* and *Rochdale,* the explicit permission to use the stage of pregnancy to render one incompetent has yet to be overruled, thus allowing for its potential application in subsequent cases. Coupled with the fact that applications for enforced caesareans have been granted in all reported cases of the UK to date, there is an undeniable presence of some degree of paternalism in the judiciary. As keenly observed by Cahill, "[t]here is evidently a distinct difference between accepting someone as competent and actually acceding to their decision making".[67] To this end, this article concludes that the caesarean cases have wandered into in an illusion of autonomy, implicitly making pregnant women a new class of incompetent adults.

---

[64] Susan Bewley, "Restricting the Freedom of Pregnant Women" in Donna Dickenson, *Maternal Fetal Ethics* (Cambridge: Cambridge University Press, 2002), 131-145.

[65] John Harris, "The Survival Lottery" [1975] 50 *Philosophy* 81.

[66] Emily Jackson, Medical Law: Text, Cases and Materials (3rd edn; Oxford: Oxford University Press, 2013), 218.

[67] Cahill, 496.

7. Bibliography

Table of statutes

Mental Capacity Act 2005
Mental Health Act 1983

Table of cases

Great Western Hospitals NHS Foundation Trust v AA and others [2014] EWHC 132
In Re AC (1987) 533 A.2d 611
NHS Trust and others v FG [2014] EWCOP 30
Norfolk and Norwich Healthcare NHS Trust v W [1997] 1 FCR 269
R v Collins, ex parte S [1998] 3 All ER 673
Re AA [2012] EWHC 4378
Re C (Adult: Refusal of Treatment) [1994] 2 FCR 151
Re E [2012] EWHC 1639
Re F (in utero) [1998] Fam 122
Re MB (An Adult: Medical Treatment) [1997] 2 FCR 541
Re S (Adult: Refusal of Treatment) [1992] 4 All ER 671
Re T (Adult: Refusal of Treatment) [1992] 3 WLR 782
Rochdale Healthcare NHS Trust v C [1997] 1 FCR 274
Sidaway v Bethlem Royal Hospital Governors [1985] 1 All ER 643
Wyatt v Curtis [2003] EWCA Civ 1779

Table of European Court of Human Rights cases

Paton v United Kingdom [1980] 3 EHRR 408

Books

Bentham, J., *A Fragment on Government* (London 1776)
Bewley, S., "Restricting the Freedom of Pregnant Women". In Dickenson, D., *Maternal Fetal Ethics*. Cambridge: Cambridge University Press, 2002.
Harris, J., *The Value of Life: An Introduction to Medical Ethics*. First published 1985; Routledge, 1990.
Jackson, E., *Medical Law: Text, Cases and Materials*. 3rd edition, Oxford: Oxford University Press, 2013.
Mill, J. S., On Liberty. Oxford: Oxford University Press, 1859.
Royal College of Obstetricians and Gynaecologists, *A Consideration of the Law and Ethics in Relation to Court-Authorized Obstetric Interventions*. London, 1994.

Scheffler, S., *The Rejection of Consequentialism*. Oxford: Oxford University Press, 1982.

Tingle, J. and Cribb, A., *Nursing Law and Ethics*. 4th edn, Wiley-Blackwell 2013.

Scott, R., *Rights, Duties and the Body: Law and Ethics of the Maternal-Fetal Conflict*. Hart, 2002.

Wells, C., "On the Outside Looking In: Perspectives on Enforced Caesareans". In Sheldon, S. & Thomson, M., *Feminist Perspectives on Health Care Law*. Cavendish, 1998.

Journal Articles

Cahill, H., "An Orwellian Scenario: Court Ordered Caesarean Section and Women's Autonomy" [1999] 6 Nursing Ethics 494.

Dalton, K. J., "Refusal of Interventions to Protect the Life of the Viable Fetus – a Case-Based Transatlantic Overview" [2006] 74 Modern Law Journal 16.

Draper, H., "Women, Forced Caesareans and Antenatal Responsibilities" [1996] 22 Journal of Medical Ethics 327.

Gies, L., Contesting the Rule of Emotions? The Press and Enforced Caesareans" [2000] 9 SLS 515.

Harris, J., "The Survival Lottery" [1975] 50 Philosophy 81.

Knopoff, K. A., "Can a Pregnant Woman Morally Refuse Fetal Surgery" [1991] 79 Cal. L. Rev. 499.

Maclean, A., "Caesarean Sections, Competence and the Illusion of Autonomy" [1999] 1 WebJCLI.

Michalowski, S., "Court-Authorised Caesarean Sections – The End of a Trend" [1999] 62 Modern Law Review 115.

Plomer, A., "Judicially Enforced Caesareans and the Sanctity of Life" [1997] 26 Anglo-American Law Review 235.

Priaulx, N., "Rethinking Progenitive Conflict: Why Reproductive Autonomy Matters" [2008] 16 Modern Law Review 169.

Stern, K., "Court-Ordered Caesarian Sections: In Whose Interests?" [1993] 56 Modern Law Review 238.

Thorpe, M. A., "Consent for Caesarean Section: Part 1 Development of the Law" [2000] May Catholic Medical Quarterly 8.

Widdett, C. & Thomson, M., "Justifying Treatment and Other Stories" [1997] 5 *FLS* 77.

Websites

National Health Service, 'How To Make a Birth Plan' (5 February 2015) <http://www.nhs.uk/Conditions/pregnancy-and-baby/pages/how-to-make-birth-plan.aspx#close> accessed 9 October 2015.

Misusing Drugs and Misapplying Paternalism: Injecting Portuguese Decriminalisation into the UK Justice System

Ellen Wright and Kate Harker[†]

This article outlines the criminalisation of drug possession in the UK, with reference to the Misuse of Drugs Act 1971, and discusses the inadequacies of criminalisation. It presents the theoretical concept of paternalism and the sub-concepts of soft and hard paternalism. These are compared in order to illustrate the current legislative situation in theoretical terms and to provide a suitable backdrop to advocate for the decriminalisation of drug possession on the basis of the un-paternalistic harm such criminalisation causes. The particular social consequences an individual may currently face as a result of an approach based on criminalisation are articulated. The reforms made in Portugal, regarding the decriminalisation of drug possession, are examined in detail and the suitability of introducing such reforms under UK legislation are assessed. Using the evidence gained from the reforms made in Portugal this paper advocates for the decriminalisation of drug possession in the UK, with the view to introducing a softer paternalistic approach. The connotations of decriminalisation are briefly discussed, with legalisation being dismissed as an option, and submissions are made for an approach that places a focus on healthcare and education in place of criminal sanctions.

Keywords: Drugs, Paternalism, Decriminalisation, Portugal, Reform

---

[†] Ellen Wright and Kate Harker are LLM graduates from Teesside University, Middlesborough, UK.

1. INTRODUCTION

In light of revelations made by a number of Police Commissioners that they no longer consider low level drug use a priority,[1] a petition calling for the complete legalisation of cannabis receiving over 150,000 signatures in under a week,[2] and Aodhán Ó Ríordáin, Minister of State for the National Drugs Strategy in Northern Ireland, outlining his plans for research into a more relaxed approach to drug-taking, there is little doubt that UK drug laws are under extensive scrutiny. The tide of opinion is no longer firmly in favour of harsher criminalisation approaches; it is now starting to change as people see the benefits of a more drug-tolerant society. This piece will raise concerns with the State's unwavering adherence to paternalism, insofar as it relies on this – protection of the person – to justify criminal sanctions for low level drugs crime. This paper argues that the qualities encompassed within the theory of paternalism do not correlate harmoniously with the laws that govern the misuse of drugs in the UK. While paternalism has proved effective in protecting individuals from physical harm in a variety of situations,[3] the physical and meta-physical destruction that stems from the misuse of drugs is arguably being exacerbated by a misguided application of a paternalism that favours criminalisation over protection. This piece will examine the theoretical principles of paternalism before examining its troubling relationship with the Misuse of Drugs Act 1971 and the changes that the application of the concept must undergo in order to properly protect some of the UK's most vulnerable citizens. A cautionary note is added that this piece will discuss such issues solely in relation to the possession of controlled substances, and not the intent to supply or traffic such substances.

---

[1] Damien Gayle, 'Police won't target pot smokers and small-scale growers, say commissioners' (*The Guardian*, 22 July 2015) < http://www.theguardian.com/society/2015/jul/22/police-wont-target-pot-smokers-small-scale-growers-commissioners > Accessed 3 September 2015.

[2] Christopher Hooton, 'UK weed legalisation petition hits 150,000 signatures, will get Parliament debate date in September' (*The Independent*, 27 July 2015), < http://www.independent.co.uk/news/uk/uk-weed-legalisation-hits-150000-signatures-will-get-parliament-debate-date-in-two-days-10417757.html > Accessed 14 August 2015.

[3] Consider legislation passed requiring the wearing of a seatbelt, banning smoking indoors and prohibiting the use of a hand held mobile phone whilst driving. The introduction of each of these was based on paternalistic motivations (to an extent), and each has proved successful in terms of protecting the individual from themselves.

1. PATERNALISM AND ITS INEXTRICABLE LINK WITH THE MISUSE OF DRUGS ACT 1971

There is a clear link between the concept of paternalism and the illegality of controlled substances, as outlined under the Misuse of Drugs Act 1971. Reflected in the regulations regarding the wearing of seat belts,[4] is the core principle of paternalism; the parent-like dictation of the actions an individual is obliged, or not in the case of drug misuse, to take in order to prevent the individual coming to harm. Describing the concept of paternalism, Feinberg outlines that

> …it is always a good reason in support of a prohibition that it is probably necessary to prevent harm (physical, psychological or economic) to the actor himself and there is probably no other means that is equally effective at no greater cost to other values.[5]

There is little debate amongst academics that the concept of paternalism concerns the protection or, at very least, the perceived protection of individuals existing under a paternalistic entity with the concept finding its application in the sacrifice of individual autonomy.

It ought to be noted that paternalism is by no means an unmoving concept that merely dictates our rule of law according to a stringent set of criteria that outlines the dangerous and the safe. Paternalism is a free moving, flexible concept that can take a variety of forms and enjoys an immeasurable scale of applicability. First, it may be of benefit to offer a fleeting insight into the sub-concept of soft paternalism. The theoretical application of soft paternalism is wholly dependent on "*whether the person being interfered with is acting voluntarily and knowledgably.*"[6] For instance, if an individual who was lacking in mental capacity[7] wished to ride her bicycle without a cycle helmet the soft paternalist would likely be inclined to prevent this action on the basis that the individual's lack of capacity prevents her from understanding the risks associated with omitting to wear the protective gear. A soft paternalist may go as far as to prevent such an action even where the individual is lacking in capacity but, nevertheless, understands the risks of not wearing a helmet while riding a bicycle; this stance is arguably formed in the idea that the lack of

[4] Road Vehicles (Construction and Use) Regulations 1986, SI 1986/1078.

[5] Joel Feinberg, *Harm to Self: The Moral Limits of the Criminal Law* (Volume 3, New York: Oxford University Press, 1986) xvii.

[6] Gerald Dworkin, 'Paternalism' (Stanford Encyclopedia of Philosophy, 4 June 2014) < http://plato.stanford.edu/entries/paternalism/ > Accessed 25 November 2015.

[7] As defined under the Mental Capacity Act 2005, s 2(1).

capacity possessed may still impede the decision-making ability of the individual regardless of any existing knowledge of danger. In stark contrast, and arguably overwhelmingly familiar in the context of UK drug policies, is the sub-concept of hard paternalism. Hard paternalism is the firm prohibition of an action that is deemed to be dangerous, regardless of whether an individual has the capacity to form a reasoned judgment.[8] Under a hard paternalistic approach, our bicycle rider would be obligated to wear a helmet despite having full capacity to understand the risks and make an informed decision. The autonomy of the individual is removed in its entirety from the, perhaps naive, perspective that individuals under the state are incapable of making decisions that are in their 'best interests'.

Such ingenuousness becomes exemplified in the apparent presumption, taken by UK policy makers, that the criminalisation of a certain activity alone will stop an individual from making the decision to consume a controlled substance. On this note, the current use of paternalism in this way will be considered. The rationale behind the implementation of criminal sanctions regarding drug use evidently relies heavily upon the principles of paternalism, specifically, hard paternalism. Under the UK justice system an individual can face up to seven years in custody if found in possession[9] of a controlled drug as defined under Section 2 of the Misuse of Drugs Act 1971.[10] This approach finds its origins in the theory of paternalism on the basis that certain controlled substances cause harm to the individual[11] and as such, the decision to consume a controlled substance is taken out of the individual's hands, through statutory provisions, in the 'best interests' of the said individual. There are clear implications, in the context of society as a whole where the misuse of controlled drugs is concerned. Namely, the devastation the use of controlled substances may cause to the families of users and the occurrence of apparent drug-related crimes such as theft. However, for the sake of clarity as far as paternalism is concerned this piece will focus solely on the negative effects suffered by the vulnerable individuals using the controlled substances.

2. THE INADEQUACIES OF CRIMINALISATION - AN INAPPROPRIATE APPLICATION OF PATERNALISM

As previously outlined, the concept of paternalism is applied in the form of legislation that restricts an individual's autonomy, preventing the individual

[8] Op. cit. no. 6.

[9] Misuse of Drugs Act 1971, s 5(2).

[10] In the context of Section 2 Misuse of Drugs Act 1971, the authors are only concerned with the possession of controlled substances.

[11] It is recognised by the authors that criminalisation also finds roots in the protection of society as a whole; the theory of which can be found in the Harm Principle.

from making decisions which the UK Government deem not to be in their 'best interests'. The use of paternalism regarding the control of prohibited substances is creating more harm than it is preventing and is thus, defying the very logic that underpins its original implementation. In effect, the current approach, far from acting in the 'best interests' of an individual, is acting as a catalyst for further harm. It ought to be recognised that the decision to criminalise a certain act or omission carries with it a heavy burden. A criminal record is not merely writing on a piece of paper; it is limited employment prospects, reduced travel opportunities and the stigma that the label of 'criminal' carries with it. It is doubtful whether handing down a criminal record has any effect on the reoffending rate of individuals found in possession of a controlled substance. In a society where the jobs market is in the hands of employers, a criminal record most certainly reduces the chances of an individual finding employment. This in turn, could leave the individual further entrapped within their habit or addiction. How can we reasonably expect an individual to change their habits if they are not provided with the tools to do so? Simply condemning the actions of an individual who consumes controlled substances, without making attempts to tackle the causing factors of such use, will not remedy the individuals using habit or reduce the level of substance abuse within our society. The restricted opportunities that the criminalisation of the possession of controlled substances presents to often vulnerable individuals is by no means the sole factor in examining the inadequacies that our current system faces.

There is a significant amount of evidence to suggest that the misuse of controlled substances does not stop at the prison gates. The Prison Reform Trust outline that "*19% of* [...] *prisoners who said they had ever used heroin reported having used heroin for the first time in a prison.*"[12] In light of such facts, the concepts of criminalisation and crime reduction seem worlds apart. The statistics outlined lead one to presume that prison may, in actuality, be a stand-alone factor in encouraging individuals to develop a penchant for 'harder' drugs. It is widely recognised that heroin is one of the most dangerous and addictive drugs on the streets of the UK[13] and the statistical assertion that individuals in the prison system are being introduced to such danger after passing through the criminal justice system without doubt shines a blindingly bright light on the inadequacies of criminalisation. Not only does heroin cause significantly more harm to the human body in terms of the effects it has when consumed, in comparison with other controlled substances

[12] Prison Reform Trust, 'Prison the Facts' < http://www.prisonreformtrust.org.uk/Portals/0/Documents/Prisonthefacts.pdf >, 7, Accessed 3 October 2015.

[13] A. B. Bucknall, J. R. Robertson, 'Deaths of Heroin Users in a General Practice Population' (1986) 36(284) Journal of the Royal College of General Practitioners 120.

of lower classifications such as cannabis, but heroin also runs increased risks for the user in terms of the viruses that can be contracted intravenously. Jurgens, Ball and Verster outline that the "use of non-sterile injecting equipment in prison was found to be the most important independent determinant of HIV infection."[14] Evidence of such magnitude cannot simply be ignored in favour of continuing under the current approach. When assessing the evident failure in the reduction of controlled substance abuse under the Misuse of Drugs Act combined with the serious health implications that the use of such substances may cause, an alternative approach with a focus on health care becomes an idea worthy of contemplation. The illegalisation of the possession of controlled substances on the basis of paternalistic protection has, without a doubt, failed.

This contention finds further support in the fact that controlled substances under the Misuse of Drugs Act are arguably become increasingly attractive under criminalisation. Rather than deterring people from using controlled substances, criminalisation may be having the opposite effect, portraying the habit in a more desirable light to vulnerable individuals within our society. Coleman and Hendry comment that the current criminalisation of controlled substances makes drug-taking appear to be appealing because it creates "the thrill of illegality" and "audience-controlled risk".[15] Amongst certain groups in society, it seems almost inevitable that this would be the case; curiosity, rebellion and kudos all combine to make drug-taking an attractive prospect. At a time when drugs are readily accessible, and are arguably becoming ingrained in our society as part of wider culture,[16] it is certainly troubling that criminalisation raises this additional layer of concern. Perhaps more so troubling, is the political landscape that has allowed the detrimental, and socially inflammatory, criminalisation of controlled substances to rumble on unhindered for so long. The authors concur with Hickman who wrote:

> [D]rug policy is, in the first instance, made for those who do not, and are not likely to take drugs. It is aimed at economically secure, mainstream voters whose chief concern is to keep themselves and especially their children off drugs. Politicians know this and, from a purely utilitarian perspective that is common across the political spectrum, strict anti-drug

---

[14] R Jurgens, A Ball, A Verster, 'Interventions to Reduce HIV Transmission Related to Injecting Drug Use in Prison' (2009) 9(1) The Lancet 57, 58.

[15] John C Coleman and Leo B Hendry, *The Nature of Adolescence* (Third Edition, London: Routledge, 1990) 128.

[16] Ibid.

> measures are good policy because they bring in votes, which is what they are designed to do.[17]

Tangled within Hickman's submission is a glimpse at the troublingly misapplied theory of paternalism discussed earlier in this piece. The core principle behind the application of paternalism is the protection of an individual from their own, potentially dangerous, decisions; theoretically, paternalism is not a two-way street whereby paternalistic policies will only be implemented if popular with the voting public. This is perhaps the ultimate logical flaw within the criminalisation of controlled substances. If we were to wholeheartedly adopt the principles behind the criminalisation of controlled substances then surely, alcohol and tobacco would be as illegal as a bag of heroin. Yet, in what is potentially an attempt to avoid an unsettled scenario not dissimilar from 1920s prohibition in America, such substances have not been criminalised and this unquestionably boils down to public opinion. Disappointingly but unsurprisingly, politics and paternalism have become entwined and the criminalisation of drug-misuse has followed. However, it is proposed that limits on public spending may dissolve this relationship.

When observed from a financial perspective, the current situation appears progressively unsustainable and therefore inadequate. It is no secret that public sector funding in the UK has undergone stringent cutbacks. Due to the restrictions bearing down on our public finances decisions of necessity will need to be made where the spending of public money is concerned. The recent disclosures made by police commissioners such as Ron Hogg and Alan Charles are arguably indicative of the acute economic pressure being placed on our public services.[18] Determining whether limited resources will be best applied to the prevention of violent crime or personal drug use the decision is far from a 'Sophie's choice' situation. When considered in conjunction with evidence that clearly suggests the criminalisation of controlled drug users is doing little to prevent the reoffending rates of such individuals, the use of limited public funds in this way seems all the more illogical. The inadequate adoption of paternalism mixed with a difficult financial situation is a recipe for failure, as such alternative approaches to the treatment of those who consume controlled substances ought to be examined.

---

[17] Timothy A Hickman, 'Why Strict Drugs Laws Work (And Why They Do Not)' (2010) 2(4) Amsterdam Law Forum < http://amsterdamlawforum.org/article/view/160/328 > Accessed 10 August 2015.

[18] Damien Gayle, 'Police won't target pot smokers and small-scale growers, say commissioners' (*The Guardian*, 22 July 2015), < http://www.theguardian.com/society/2015/jul/22/police-wont-target-pot-smokers-small-scale-growers-commissioners > Accessed 3 September 2015.

3. Portugal Leads the Way - An Alternate Approach Towards Drug-Taking

The methods of decriminalisation used by Portugal offer brighter prospects where drug use is concerned. Portugal, like the UK, faced issues with increasing drug use,[19] within a society which had come to accept drug-taking as almost the norm. As a result, they opted for widespread reform; reform which has gone on to attract attention from countries all around the world. Portugal took the bold step of removing drug-taking from the scope of criminal law altogether, at a time when the trend was leaning towards harsher criminalisation approaches. In 2001, Portuguese legislators expressly decriminalised drugs, with much success in the interim period. It has to be noted that this step was, however, not taken in isolation; it was part of a wider policy change. Serious investment was made in treatment and harm reduction services, and extensive changes were made to health and social policy.

3.1. The Approach: A Possibility for England?

The approach taken in Portugal – and heralded as a significant success[20] – is to deal with the purchase, possession, and consumption of *all*[21] drugs for personal use[22] as administrative violations only. What this means for drugs regulation in Portugal is that any persons suspected of committing the above are dealt with outside the realm of Portuguese criminal law. They are processed not by the courts, but by administrative panels set up specifically to deal with low level drugs violations, and they decide what sanctions, if any, to impose. This exemplifies a 'softer' approach towards drug-taking, when we consider the policy trend towards harsher criminalisation approaches, even at user level, over the past thirty years. Arguably, paternalistic motivations are more noticeable from this softer approach to drug-taking, exuding a more optimistic undertone. The Portuguese Government was very much motivated by health-based concerns when implementing the new model; the country wanted very much to redirect the focus to prevention, whilst also providing greater access to medical treatment for individuals who sought help with their

---

[19] In particular, Portugal faced real issues with the increasing prevalence of intravenous heroin use.

[20] If we measure Portugal's success by those who are pushing for repeal, there are few.

[21] Al psychoactive drugs, including cocaine and heroin are covered by the legislation. The Portuguese system does not draw a distinction between so called 'soft' and 'hard' drugs.

[22] Defined as the average individual quantity sufficient for 10 days' usage for one person. (Decriminalization of Drug Use Act). Note that criminal sanctions remain possible for those growing, trafficking or selling illicit drugs.

addiction.[23] In other words, it implemented a paternalistic system, free from political motives, which aimed to truly act in the 'best interests' of the drug user. The authors would suggest that this is where the disconnection currently lies within the English system; while the State justifies criminalisation on the basis of protection of the person (paternalism), it puts nothing in place to actually 'protect' that person. It relies on the deterrence model; the concept that people will refrain from drug use and therefore self-harm because of a fear of a possible criminal record. This may deter people from consuming controlled substances in the first place, but what effect does it have on those who take such drugs and go onto become addicted? Arguably, it has none. The English system needs to evolve. It needs to recognise the person most in need of help in this equation – the drug user – and relax its approach to criminalisation so as to protect the health and wellbeing of such vulnerable individuals.

It ought to be noted on behalf of those fearful of a step in an alternative direction that, if the UK were to adopt such an approach, controlled substances would not be legalised, but instead decriminalised, insofar as they were purchased or consumed for personal use. With decriminalisation, prohibition would remain the guiding rule, as is the case in Portugal. However, as opposed to facing criminal sanctions like imprisonment, offenders would be subject to non-criminal sanctions like banning orders and treatment requirements only. A seemingly drastic change, this is exactly the type of holistic approach to dealing with drug-taking that the authors advocate for in England. The State has to at some point recognise the benefit of medical help and guidance over penalisation, particularly given the intrinsic problems inherent in UK prison facilities as discussed above.

One would be forgiven for thinking that the complete removal of criminal sanctions would be incompatible with the aim of furthering the health of our drug-taking population. Indeed, increased drug use, a further increase in HIV incidence and a breakdown in society were all fears cited prior to implementation of the Portuguese model.[24] If however, we take this model as an example, we can see that actually a lot of these concerns are unfounded; based more on fear than fact. What is required is a major shift in the way that people perceive drug-taking, so that people see drug-takers as individuals in need of medical treatment, and not as criminals deserving of punishment.

[23] Glenn Greenwald, *Drug Decriminalization in Portugal: Lessons for Creating Fair and Successful Drug Policies* (Cato Institute, 2007) 7 < http://object.cato.org/sites/cato.org/files/pubs/pdf/greenwald_whitepaper.pdf> accessed 30 November 2015.

[24] One impassioned comment was: "There will be planeloads of students heading for [Portugal] to smoke marijuana and take a lot worse, knowing we won't put them in jail. We promise sun, beaches and any drug you like." [Quoted in Daniel McGrory, 'Portugal Police Won't Arrest Drug Takers' *Times* (London, 14 July 2001)].

This is encapsulated in the change that the Portuguese system has undergone. They now operate a referral system, arrest no longer existing as a possibility, whereby people found to be in possession of illicit substances are referred to Dissuasion Commissions. Dissuasion Commissions are regional panels made up of three experienced professionals; one of whom must have a legal background, and at least one of the other two a medical or social services type background. Their role is less concerned with punishment, and more with encouraging those dependent on drugs to seek medical treatment for their addiction.[25] The key word here is *encourage*, since they will not compel dependent users to enter a treatment facility; their aim is for users to make that choice for themselves and to voluntarily engage in treatment thereafter.[26] The emphasis is firmly on providing access to medical treatment, though a wider range of sanctions is available, including suspension of the right to practice as a licensed professional, the termination of public benefits and a ban on where one can go and/or with whom one can associate with. This is a provision for those categorised as addicts only. For users who are not deemed to be dependent on banned substances the system differs. Such individuals may receive a fine or a non-pecuniary penalty which may be as little as a warning, or, for non-dependent drug users with no prior offences, no sanction at all. In such instances, case proceedings will be 'provisionally suspended'.

It is perhaps worth mentioning that the police are still involved in the regulation of controlled substances, irrespective of the fact that they can no longer make an arrest. They issue the citation that will set this administrative process in motion.[27] It is suggested that the role of the Portuguese police force in the regulation of drugs has, in actuality, increased since their power to arrest was revoked. The case is put forward by some that:

> …police officers…are more inclined to act when they see drug usage now than they were before decriminalization, as they believe that the treatment options offered to such users are far more effective than turning users into criminals (who, even under the criminalization scheme, were typically back on the street the next day, but without real treatment options).[28]

If this is to be believed, it exemplifies a radical shift in the way that drug users are perceived in Portugal. It shows them recognised by members of wider society as individuals in need of medical help, rather than as criminals.

---

[25] Op. cit., no. 24, 6.

[26] Op. cit., no. 23, 9.

[27] Note that referrals can come from physicians as well. Given the confidential nature of the doctor/patient relationship and the breach of confidence this would necessitate though, this would likely be a rare case.

[28] Op. cit., no. 23, 9.

Certainly, such a shift in opinion will have come about as a result of the wide scale changes mentioned above. However, the smaller changes made to the system cannot go unmentioned, for some of these may have had just as much of an impact. Most notably, the hearing, brought with regard to substances misuse, is designed to be devoid of all the things you would typically associate with a criminal trial. Commission members are not placed on a pedestal in the same way as judges; they will dress informally and will sit on the same level as the offender. Respect for the offender is also a central tenet. Offenders are entitled to complete confidentiality in relation to all proceedings, such that they can even request that notice of the proceedings is not sent to their home address. This is a marked difference from how drug users would be dealt with under a strictly criminal system.

3.2. The Portuguese Approach in Practice

"[J]udged by virtually every metric, the Portuguese decriminalization framework has been a resounding success." This is the impassioned statement made in the Cato Institute's 2009 report into the Portuguese decriminalisation framework.[29] This shows the Portuguese methods of decriminalisation to be a success, and certainly there are others who would concur. Thornton emphasises that "Portugal has the second lowest death rate from illegal drugs in all of Europe after experiencing one of the worst rates with prohibition",[30] demonstrating that a strong correlation may be drawn between the concept of decriminalisation and the protection of society as a whole.[31] A cautionary note is, however, added that, some sources provide an alternative picture of how effective reform has been.[32] This can be affected by the way that the data is gathered and the metric used. Moreover, there is an inevitable difficulty to collecting data on drug-taking.

One picture presented though, is that none of the fears cited prior to decriminalisation have actually materialised. Portugal has not become a hub for youngsters wishing to take drugs legally, nor has drug-taking escalated out

---

[29] Op. cit., no. 23, 1.

[30] Mark Thornton, 'Portugal's Experiment in Drug Decriminalization Has Been a Success' (*Mises Daily*, 2015) < https://mises.org/library/portugal%E2%80%99s-experiment-drug-decriminalization-has-been-success > Accessed on 25 November 2015

[31] This is a notion further emphasised by Zeeshan Aleem in, '14 Years After Decriminalizing Drugs Here's What Portugal Looks Like' (*Policy. Mic*, 11 February 2015) < http://mic.com/articles/110344/14-years-after-portugal-decriminalized-all-drugs-here-s-what-s-happening#.dGZIBu2FS > Accessed on 25 November 2015.

[32] The policy decision has been termed 'a disastrous failure' in M Pinto Coelho's, *The 'Resounding Success' of Portuguese Drug Policy: The Power of an Unattractive Fallacy* (Lisboa, Associação para uma Portugal livre de drogas, 2010).

of control. In fact, the indication is that drug-taking is no longer the uncontrollable social problem that it once was. Data from the National Statistics Institute shows a decrease in drug-related and drug-induced deaths following decriminalisation.[33] Such a decrease would suggest that the necessary provision is now there for drug-users to receive the help that they need, and that via the administrative system, drug-users are now directed towards appropriate treatment facilities. Another possible cause of this decline (a bold to statement to make admittedly) is that perhaps fewer people are now taking up the habit. This is not unthinkable when we know that criminalisation is coexistent with the glamorisation of drugs. As discussed previously, 'the thrill of illegality' is one of the influential factors in people experimenting with drugs in the first place.[34] But, regardless of whether it is true that fewer people are taking up drugs, Portugal has by no means plunged into the drugs crisis predicted prior to the new regime.[35]

Fears cited regarding the rampant spread of HIV have also proved false. It is reported that general infection rates have remained stable since decriminalisation, and that in the five years following the implementation of this new model, there was actually a decline in the percentage of drug users among newly infected HIV positive individuals.[36] Set in the context of Portugal's drug problem prior to decriminalisation this is all the more noteworthy. For prior to 2001, Portugal was renowned for its high level of problem drug use, particularly intravenous heroin use which carries with it inherent risks of HIV, AIDs and hepatitis. In light of the apparent success that can be seen following Portugal's shift in policy, serious consideration ought to be given to a new, UK, approach to the use of controlled drugs.

4. ALTERNATIVE APPLICATION: A NEW APPROACH TO ILLICIT DRUG USE

Instead of viewing drug use as a weakness of character that erodes our seemingly reasonable society we ought to view the use of drugs, in addicts and non-addicts alike, as an issue of medical concern as our first and foremost priority. Surely, harm would be more successfully reduced if we were to

---

[33] Cited in Caitlin Hughes and Alex Stevens, 'A resounding success or a disastrous failure: Re-examining the interpretation of evidence on the Portuguese decriminalisation of illicit drugs' (2012) 31 Drug and Alcohol Review 101, 107-108.
[34] John C Coleman and Leo B Hendry, *The Nature of Adolescence* (Third Edition, London: Routledge), 128.
[35] Zeeshan Aleem, '14 Years After Decriminalising All Drugs, Here's What Portugal Looks Like' *(Policy.Mic,* 11 February 2015) < http://mic.com/articles/110344/14-years-after-portugal-decriminalized-all-drugs-here-s-what-s-happening > Accessed 9 September 2015.
[36] *Op. cit.* no. 23, 15-16.

target the wellbeing of the individual as opposed to simply condemning the individual. It is fervently argued that a person cannot combat their drug use if they are not given the tools and motivation to do so.

As discussed above, the hard paternalistic approach that is being implemented at present is unquestionably failing in its mission to prevent drug misuse within the UK. It is submitted that a new health-based approach to drug use that allows individuals to receive treatment and education without fear of criminalisation would be far more effective in the reduction of drug use within the UK. This piece is by no means advocating for the full legalisation of controlled substances, it is simply encouraging the decriminalisation of controlled substances in order to open the gate to harm prevention that is non-existent under the current state of affairs. At this point, it is perhaps fitting to note the difference between the decriminalisation and the legalisation of drugs. Legalisation in the eyes of the authors refers to a state of affairs where everything from the sale and distribution to the consumption of controlled substances is no longer a criminal offence. Decriminalisation, in the alternative, refers to a state of affairs where individuals found to be in possession of a controlled substance would not face criminal sanctions – where the controlled drug is for personal use. The statutes and sanctions governing the sale and distribution of controlled substances would, in relation to both, remain relatively unchanged.

It is submitted that the decriminalisation of controlled substances, with an alternative emphasis on healthcare and education, would most certainly produce many benefits. Allowing individuals to seek help for their addictions without the stigma and risks associated with a criminal record hanging over them may result in more people tackling their addictions and thus reducing the number of individuals consuming controlled substances. It may be argued that not everyone who consumes controlled substances is an addict and this is a point accepted by the authors. This is where the provision of education regarding such substances would come into play. If we were to educate individuals on the risks associated with the various controlled substances further use may decline. It goes without saying that such a reduction may not occur and use may continue unabated. It is however submitted, that criminalisation has undoubtedly failed in curbing the use of controlled substances and thus, there is little to lose by taking a tentative step in an alternate direction. Effectively, it is proposed that by taking a soft paternalistic approach and giving individuals who take controlled substances the tools to make more informed decisions, as opposed to blindly banning such substances, the attraction of using such substances may reduce. Additionally, our law enforcers may perhaps be more inclined to intervene in instances of controlled substances being taken for personal use if the individual is to be seen as a patient rather than a criminal as demonstrated by the changing attitudes of Portugal.

The authors by no means purport to be economists but it is considered that the funding for a health-based approach could be found in the pot of savings made by a criminal justice system that is free from those who have been found in possession of a controlled substance. The Prison Reform Trust have outlined that "the average cost of a prison place in England and Wales for the financial year 2011-12 is £37,648."[37] A system which targets the addictions of drug users and educates those who find themselves tempted by controlled substances will not only reduce the number of people consuming illegal drugs but, will also reduce the level of drug-related crimes such as theft. Naturally, it is by no means submitted that such an approach would be a success for every person to pass through its doors however, given the palpable inadequacies of the current approach there is plenty of room for a new line of attack.

5. Conclusion

To summarise, the current approach taken by the UK is wholly inadequate. The Misuse of Drugs Act 1971 illustrates the hard line paternalistic model used by the UK as far as drug-users are concerned and such criminalisation, far from affording protection to potentially vulnerable individuals, actively causes further harm. Reduced employment prospects and stigmatisation mean that such offenders will be pushed deeper into the destructive cycle they have found themselves in. Quite often, it is help rather than punishment that drug-users require and this is an ideal that has been recognised by Portugal in their reform of drug policy. The decriminalisation of drug-use in Portugal has not created a drug-use epidemic, nor has it caused a leap in drug-related crime or an economic meltdown. What is has created, is a system whereby individuals with drug addictions can take back their lives to become productive members of society and young people who make a mistake do not have their opportunities in life slashed as a result. To conclude, the authors submit that a soft paternalistic approach in the UK which is based on the Portuguese model, with an emphasis on wellbeing and education away from the criminal justice system, will significantly reduce risk of ham to some of the most vulnerable individuals within our society.

---

[37] Prison Reform Trust, 'Prison the Facts' < http://www.prisonreformtrust.org.uk/Portals/0/Documents/Prisonthefacts.pdf >, 7, Accessed 3 October 2015

Agamben's State of Exception in Context: A Critical Analysis with Regard to Post-9/11 Jurisprudence

Stefanos Xenofontos[†]

The traditional juristic definition of the sovereign as 'he who decides on the exception', which has been introduced by the social and legal philosopher Carl Schmitt in Political Theology, *arguably constitutes the* clef de voûte *which enables us to underpin the philosophy of the state of exception. Whereas exceptions of law under ordinary circumstances operate within a predetermined constitutional order, which provides guidelines on how these situations are to be dealt with, a state of emergency does not need an existing legal order to function. Within this context, the sovereign has the ultimate power to transcend the legal order and impose such measures as deemed necessary to confront the crisis and re-establish order and stability within the nation, usually by invoking the 'public good'. In Agamben's work, the concept of necessity has a fundamental role in establishing the state of exception. It has been acknowledged that 'necessity creates its own law' and, occasionally, it constitutes the main justification for governments to implement their executive orders, albeit the transgression of the law. In the aftermath of 9/11, the United States faced an exceptional situation of national emergency in which it was deemed urgent to confront a new kind of threat by any necessary means. More than a decade on, and following similar events in other Western countries, it can be argued that the global legal and political order of the 21st century has changed dramatically, manifesting, what it is now evident, a permanent state of emergency.*

Keywords: political theory, state of exception, 'force-of-law', post-9/11 jurisprudence

[†] LLM student in Public International Law, University of Leicester.

1. INTRODUCTION

Following the terrorist attacks on 11 September, the United States faced an unprecedented situation of prolonged national emergency in which it was deemed urgent to deploy all necessary means to confront a new kind of threat. More than a decade on, and after experiencing similar outrageous acts of terrorism and extremism in other Western countries, it can be argued that the global legal and political order of the 21st century has changed dramatically. Through a historical and legal contextualisation of state of exception, Giorgio Agamben argues that this powerful strategy, which was originally introduced as a provisional measure, has been developed into the dominant paradigm of contemporary government and has the potential to inevitably transform democracies into totalitarian states.[1] In analysing Agamben's theory, this paper aims to demonstrate, through examples found in post-9/11 practices, how the sovereign can extend its power and transcend the rule of law in the name of the 'public good'.

The article is divided into four parts. In the first part, the author seeks to explore the idea of state of exception in its political and juridical context, by giving prominence to the structures of sovereignty, life and law, as it has been developed in modern constitutionalism. The no-man's land between juridical law and politics in which the state of exception operates will be better analysed through the concept of the 'force-of-law' and its spectral existence, as illustrated in Agamben's *State of Exception.*[2] The second part of the paper focuses on the practical application of the state of exception in contemporary politics, by providing examples of practices established in the USA and the UK, with particular reference to post-9/11 jurisprudence. Essentially, it will be demonstrated how and, most importantly, why the global political and legal order has changed since then. In the following part, the author examines the legality of executive measures imposed in a state of exception and the importance as well as the effectiveness of the judiciary in challenging and controlling the government's extended powers. Finally, the immanent necessity of this paradigm of government for the proper function of the modern society will be critically evaluated and questioned through the prism of democracy and the rule of law.

---

[1] Giorgio Agamben, *The State of Exception* (University of Chicago, 2005).

[2] Ibid., 32-34.

2. *NECESSITAS LEGEM NON HABET* (NECESSITY HAS NO LAW)[3]

In conceptualising the term of 'state of exception', Agamben makes extensive references to Carl Schmitt, who introduced this political phenomenon in his writings in *Political Theology*.[4] The juristic definition of the sovereign as 'he who decides on the exception' [5] is arguably the keystone which enables us to underpin the philosophy of the state of exception. In this context, a state of exception is presented as a kind of severe economic or political disturbance that requires the application of extraordinary measures.[6] A situation of emergency is, thus, created, in which an extreme peril or danger threatens the existence of the state. Whereas exceptions of law under ordinary circumstances operate within a predetermined constitutional order, which provides guidelines on how these situations are to be dealt with, a state of emergency does not need an existing legal order to function.[7] The sovereign, who can either be one person or the executive branch of the government as a whole, has the ultimate power to transcend the legal order and impose such measures as deemed necessary to confront the crisis and re-establish order and stability within the nation. Agamben argues that although the term 'state of exception' is widely common in German theory, terms such as 'stage of siege' and 'emergency powers' have been used to describe similar situations of crisis in other European countries.[8]

Historical examples presented in *State of Exception*, such as the medieval Roman *iustitium*, the French *state of siège* or the case of the Nazi State and the suspension of certain articles of the Weimar Constitution, have shown that a set of political and juridical phenomena must exist simultaneously in order for a state of exception to be imposed.[9] First of all, the sovereign rule expands its own constitutional powers and issues executive decrees having the force of law to confront the danger threatening the security of the nation. In the same context, an order for the suspension of the established juridical order is made and, consequently, all constitutional norms which protect individual rights and liberties and guarantee all the necessary checks and balances, which are normally to be found in a democratic system of government, are not enforced. Essentially, the democratic principle of the separation of powers has ceased to exist, since the role of the legislature is now limited to ratifying the decrees issued by the executive, without having the power to hold the government into account. Due process, civil liberties, fundamental rights and other

---

[3] Ibid., 24.
[4] Carl Schmitt, *Political Theology* (MIT Press, 1985).
[5] Ibid., 5.
[6] Ibid.
[7] Ibid., 30.
[8] Agamben, 4-5.
[9] Agamben, 3, 4-5, 47.

constitutional protections for the citizens are also suspended. An 'emptiness of law' and a 'zone of anomie' [10] are, thus, created, where the executive, as the sovereign of the state, is delegated a legislative power that should normally rest with parliament.[11]

Agamben, in explaining the relation between state of exception and law, argues that this phenomenon is neither external nor internal to the juridical order.[12] It rather concerns law's threshold where the borders of the legal and the political blur with each other, creating an 'ambiguous, uncertain, borderline fringe, at the intersection of the legal and the political'.[13] The suspension of the legal order does not mean its abolition; the law's restrictions are exceptionally disregarded 'without thereby ceasing to remain in force' and in a juridical sense, an order still exists.[14] This separation of the norm from its application takes place in order for the constitution to protect its own existence and make its effective regulation possible. Remarkably, Agamben chooses to explain this zone of anomie through the concept of the 'force-of-law' and its spectral existence. In a state of exception, the 'force-of-law' does not refer to the law but to those decrees and measures issued by the executive, which are not formally laws since they have not passed by the parliament, but nevertheless they are in force, as if they were laws. Therefore, a situation is formed where the norm (ie the constitution or legal order) is in force but not applied, and, on the other, acts that do not have the value of law acquire its force (force-of-law).[15]

In Agamben's work, the concept of necessity has a fundamental role in establishing the state of exception. It has been acknowledged that 'necessity creates its own law' and, occasionally, it constitutes the main justification for governments to implement their executive orders, albeit the transgression of the law. Without explicitly supporting the view that necessity has the power to render the illicit licit, Agamben points out that it can 'justify a single, specific case of transgression by means of an exception'.[16]

As we have examined the concept of state of exception as presented by Schmitt and Agamben, in the following section, we are going to examine how this political theory has been developed into the dominant paradigm of government in contemporary politics and how it has now become the rule rather than the exception, by focusing on the post-9/11 jurisprudence.

---

[10] Ibid., 6.
[11] Ibid., 7.
[12] Ibid., 23.
[13] A. Fontana, *Le droit de resistance: Du droit de resistance au devoir d'insurrection*, (Jean-Claude Zancarini ed, Paris: ENS 1999), 16.
[14] Schmitt, 137.
[15] Agamben, 37-39.
[16] Agamben, 24.

3. THE STATE OF EXCEPTION AS A PARADIGM OF CONTEMPORARY GOVERNMENT

The coordinated terrorist attacks of September 11, 2001 on the USA have been characterised as the deadliest foreign attack in the nation's modern history because of the thousands of casualties that were caused and, most importantly, the prolonged situation of exceptional insecurity in which the whole nation has come.[17] Subsequent similar events of terrorism in other Western countries and the rise of the so-called 'Islamic State', not only served to maintain the ongoing 'war on terror' but also reaffirmed Agamben's view of a permanent state of exception,[18] by allowing governments' imperatives 'of going outside the legal order in order to tackle extremely grave national dangers and threats'.[19] In this section, issues such as the detention, interrogation and prosecution of suspected terrorists, as well as security and risk prevention techniques introduced by governments will be examined. Although military interventions in Afghanistan and Iraq constitute an integral part of the 'war on terror', this concept will not be discussed, as it is regulated by the use of force and other principles of International law, thus not falling directly within the sphere of state of exception.

In the aftermath of 9/11, the president of the USA issued the Declaration of Emergency with respect to the terrorist attacks.[20] The Declaration has since been renewed on several occasions by both President Bush and President Obama in order to confront the continuing and immediate threat to national security, thus rendering the country in a permanent state of emergency, with the inevitable, under the circumstances, suspension of some constitutional provisions protecting individual liberties.[21] Notably, the U.S Senate passed the USA Patriot Act of 2001, allowing the Attorney General to authorise indefinite detentions of non-nationals and maintain into custody any alien whose activities endanger the national security of the United States.[22] Additionally, the Act permits law enforcement officers to conduct searches

---

[17] Matthew J. Morgan, *The impact of the 9/11 on Politics and War: The day that changed everything?* (Palgrave Macmillan, 2009), 200, 204, 207.

[18] Agamben, 87.

[19] Fleur Johns, 'Guantanamo Bay and the Annihilation of the Exception' (2005) 16 *EJIL* 613.

[20] 'Notice: Continuation of the National Emergency with Respect to Certain Terrorist Attacks' (*The White House,* 12 September 2007) < http://georgewbush-whitehouse.archives.gov/news/releases/2007/09/20070912-2.html > accessed 26 October 2015.

[21] 'Letter from the President on the Continuation of the National Emergency with Respect to Certain Terrorist Attacks' (*The White House*, 10 September 2010) < https://www.whitehouse.gov/the-press-office/2010/09/10/letter-president-continuation-national-emergency-with-respect-certain-te > accessed 26 October 2015.

[22] USA Patriot Act of 2001, s 412.

without warrants, gather and share intelligence information from both nationals and non-nationals on suspicion of terrorism.[23] This 'zone of anomie' becomes more apparent with the Authorization for Use of Military Force (AUMF), passed by Congress shortly after September 11, 2001. By virtue of this measure, the President has the ultimate power to 'use all necessary and appropriate force against those nations, organisations or persons he determines planned, authorized, committed, or aided the terrorist attacks'.[24]

Another characteristic illustration of a permanent state of exception is the situation created by virtue of the Detainee Treatment Act of 2005. The US Senate and President, by passing this legislation, signed away any legal protection available to prisoners held at the Guantánamo Bay detention camp, 'whose very existence is a bold illustration of legally constituted anomic space'.[25] According to the 2005 Act, 'no court, justice, or judge shall have jurisdiction to hear…an application for a writ of habeas corpus' [26] by any alien detained at Guantánamo and, consequently, nobody could bring an action against the USA regarding any aspect of their detention. Additionally, President Bush signed the Military Order of 2001, which authorised the indefinite detention of non-national terrorist suspects and their trial by military commissions.[27] By completely erasing any juridical status of the detainees[28] and classifying them as illegal enemy combatants rather than prisoners of war (whose status is protected under international humanitarian law, mainly by the Third Geneva Convention 1949 and Additional Protocol I of 1977), the government was enabled to employ more coercive interrogation techniques and violate detainees' rights to a fair trial and due process. The suspension of constitutional norms protecting civil rights at Guantanamo embodies Agamben's figure of *homo sacer,* who is subject to 'a space devoid of law…in which all legal determinations…are deactivated', drawing dramatic parallels between Guantanamo and the Nazi concentration camps.[29]

Terms of domestic spying and mass surveillance have also been very common within the daily discourse of the US National Security Strategy in relation to security and risk prevention. Under a presidential order in 2002, the National Security Agency was authorised to secretly eavesdrop US citizens without the ordinary court-approved warrants for the purpose of dealing with the new threat, hiding any violation of the right to privacy behind the 'national

---

[23] Ibid., ss 364 (3), 505-508, 701.
[24] Act codified at 115 Stat. 224 and passed as S.J.Res. 23 by the US Congress.
[25] Stephen Humphreys, 'Legalising Lawlessness: On Giorgio Agamben's State of Exception' (2006) 17 *EJIL* 677.
[26] Detainee Treatment Act of 2005, s 1005(e).
[27] Military Order of 2001, ss 1(e), 2(b) and 3(e).
[28] See the application of the notion of the 'force-of-law' as analysed further above.
[29] Agamben, 50.

security' justification.[30] The scandalous dimensions of the dragnet style data collection program, PRISM, operated by the NSA in the US and GCHQ in the UK, with which a huge amount of citizen's personal information of their daily lives has been received, even when communications were not terrorism-related, have been later fully exposed.[31] The advancement of technology in the 21st century also allowed the use of drones, which have originally been employed by the US military in operations in Afghanistan and Iraq, for domestic mass surveillance purposes by the US government, under the President's Surveillance Program.[32] Drones have been proven to be tools of great effectiveness that permit the police to surveil individuals 24/7, thus, enabling the country to be transformed into a surveillance state, or potentially into an Orwellian society, capable of serving the modern governance ends. Unsurprisingly, public concerns were raised over safeguards and accountability mechanisms that should be provided to ensure that 'law enforcement does not use drones to engage in warrantless mass surveillance', while triggering a new debate over national security and the protection of privacy.[33]

In a similar context in the UK, although the Terrorism Act 2000 aimed at combating terrorism in Northern Ireland, after 9/11, the Blair administration deemed necessary to pass a new series of stricter anti-terror legislation. Anti-Terrorism, Crime and Security Act 2001, Prevention of Terrorism Act 2005, Terrorism Act 2006 and Counter-Terrorism Act 2008 are some of the legislation implemented, granting extensive powers to the police and security services, while trading off fundamental human rights guaranteed by domestic legislation to protect national security. 'Stop and Search' by the police without reasonable suspicion, indefinite detentions without trial of foreign nationals accused of terrorist offences, pre-charge detentions, control orders and the non-implementation of due process are some of the exceptional measures

---

[30] James Risen and Eric Lichtblau, 'Bush Lets U.S. Spy on Callers Without Courts' (*The New York Times*, 16 December 2005) < http://www.nytimes.com/2005/12/16/politics/16program.html?pagewanted=all&_r=1& > accessed 23 October 2015.

[31] Edward Snowden, 'If I end up in Guantanamo, I can live with that' (*The Guardian Interviews*, 18 July 2014) < https://www.youtube.com/watch?v=L_amBkYx_Fk > accessed 23 October 2015.

[32] Carol Cratty, 'FBI uses drones for surveillance in U.S', (*CNN*, June 20 2013) < http://edition.cnn.com/2013/06/19/politics/fbi-drones/ > accessed 19 October 2015.

[33] Linda Lye, 'Easily Abused, Domestic drones raises enormous privacy concerns', (*American Civil Liberties Union*, 19 October 2012) < https://www.aclu.org/blog/speakeasy/easily-abused-domestic-drones-raise-enormous-privacy-concerns?redirect=blog/technology-and-liberty-national-security/easily-abused-domestic-drones-raise-enormous-privacy > accessed 23 October 2015.

which resulted in criticism of the government as 'one of the most authoritarian governments in living memory' which imposes 'draconian legislation'.[34]

4. THE LEGALITY OF EXECUTIVE MEASURES IN STATE OF EXCEPTION

As it has been acknowledged above, one of the most significant characteristics of the state of exception is the ultimate power of the sovereign to make decisions, which, although they are not formally laws, they acquire its 'force' and are enforced as if they were laws. According to Eichmann, in the Nazi regime, 'the words of the Fuhrer have the force of law' and because of the idea that the sovereign acts as the 'guardian of the constitution' to ensure the continuing existence of the state and, therefore, his decisions are justified and nobody can challenge or question them.[35] However, the commander-in-chief powers that have been occasionally invoked in the name of national security undermine both separation of powers and constitutional order, which, subsequently, modern democratic societies have sought to re-establish.

In assessing the legality of the state of exception through modern constitutionalism, it is to be appreciated that this phenomenon has become 'an integral part of positive law'.[36] Although Agamben has distanced his position from this view, as described above, sovereign governments justify their exceptional measures by utilising provisions of existing legislation. It is argued, therefore, that, contrary to Schmitt's principal argument that a liberal constitutional order has no law to cover the exception, the state of exception is nowadays codified in international and domestic legislation through the notion of derogation. Notably, Article 4 of the International Covenant on Civil and Political Rights (ICCPR), Article 15 of the European Convention on Human Rights (ECHR), which is also embodied in Article 15 of the Human Rights Act 1998 and Article 27 of the American Convention on Human Rights (ACHR) provide the government of each state with the power to transgress any derogable rights in order to confront a public emergency that threatens the life of the nation. Consequently, both governments of the US and the UK have invoked national security as a justification, by virtue of these derogation clauses, for violating fundamental human rights, while effectively creating a

[34] Ben Russell, 'The battle for civil liberties: Government on offensive after criticism of 'authoritarian' laws' (*The Independent*, 17 April 2012) < http://www.independent.co.uk/news/uk/politics/the-battle-for-civil-liberties-government-on-offensive-after-criticism-of-authoritarian-laws-359794.html > accessed 24 October 2015.

[35] Agamben, 38.

[36] Ibid., 23.

'double-layered constitutional system'.[37] Practices of indefinite detention, obtaining evidence by torture and warrantless privacy incursions, imposed on both sides of the Atlantic as presented above, are considered necessary by these states involved in the 'war on terror'. It is, thus, argued that judicial accountability mechanisms should not be used to challenge them.[38]

The importance of the role of the judiciary, however limited or weakened due to the executive's power in a state of exception, in controlling or restoring the legal order should not be overlooked. Significantly, the UK House of Lords in *A. v. Secretary of State for the Home Department*[39] ruled that the government's derogation from its human rights obligations were incompatible with the ECHR. The Lords held that, although there was a situation of emergency requiring derogation, the indefinite detention of foreign nationals in the Belmarsh prison without trial under the Anti-terrorism, Crime and Security Act 2001 was a disproportionate response and constituted a violation of prisoners' fundamental rights, resulting in the legislation's subsequent replacement by the Parliament. As Baroness Hale highlighted in the *Belmarsh* case 'Protecting the life of the nation is one of the first tasks of a government in a world of nation states. That does not mean that the courts could never intervene. Unwarranted declarations of emergency are a familiar tool of tyranny'.[40] In reaching this conclusion, the House of Lords was in line with the ECHR case law, which made clear that unnecessary or disproportionate derogations for reasons of national security cannot be justified.[41] Similarly, the US Supreme Court in *Rasul v. Bush* held that the government's decision to suspend the right to habeas corpus review of Guantánamo detainees was unconstitutional and, consequently, hundreds of non-nationals held at the camp indefinitely had a legal right to challenge their imprisonment.[42] The Supreme Court concluded that the state's decision for indefinite detention violated detainees' right to a fair trial and due process and their right to privacy, as provided for under the Fifth Amendment of the US Constitution as well as their rights under the Geneva Convention on prisoners of war. In this way, the judiciary showed that it can substantively intervene as well as critically examine and invalidate the decisions of the executive, restoring

---

[37] See, Tom R. Hickman, 'Between Human Rights and the Rule of Law: Indefinite detention and the derogation model of constitutionalism' (2005) 68 Modern Law Review 655, 659.

[38] Oren Gross, 'Chaos and rules: Should responses to violent crises always by constitutional?' (2011) Minnesota Public Law Research Paper No. 03-2, 1011.

[39] [2004] UKHL 56.

[40] *A v Secretary of State for the Home Department, X v Secretary of State for the Home Department*, [2005] AC 68, 172.

[41] *Lawless v. Ireland* (No.3) (App.332/57) 1961, *Ireland v. UK* (App.5310/71) 1978.

[42] U.S. 466 (2004), see also *Hamdi v. Rumsfeld* 542 U.S. 507 (2004).

fundamental principles and rights upon which democratic societies are founded.[43]

5. BALANCING HUMAN RIGHTS IN A TIME OF EMERGENCY

As it has been demonstrated, some democratic states have adopted in their constitutional order Schmitt's idea of the suspension of the rule of law by the executive as the ultimate act of sovereignty. The new political and legal order that was created as a result of the 9/11 attacks sets the basis for governments to invoke the rationale of national security as the justification for the transgression of the legal order, necessary to meet the new threat. This practice has consequently resulted to permanent exceptional measures violating fundamental human rights. The fact that the US government required its allies to stand by its side and compromise their constitutional and international commitments created the basis not only for a national state of emergency but also an international state of emergency.[44]

In the wake of 'war on terror', many Western democratic states decided that the ordinary criminal justice system was not an effective tool to deal with the new threat, thus a new national security strategy was needed, which would include stricter measures, albeit the adverse consequences on their domestic legal order. One could support the idea that the exceptional measures imposed by governments correspond to the general feeling of post-9/11 suspicion and insecurity. The more terrorist organisations continue to provoke by attacking or threatening innocent people, the more oppressive measures will be implemented by governments to make clear that the security of their citizens cannot be compromised. Arguably, the US intelligent agencies declared that applying post-9/11 anti-terrorism practices is essential to ensure national security. The FBI supports that over one hundred terrorist plots have been foiled due to the implementation of such measures[45] while, referring particularly to the necessity and effectiveness of mass surveillance practices, a NSA officer said: 'I can show you proof that the lack of this really failed and when you lose 3000 people, that proof is pretty compelling', regarding the 9/11 attacks.[46] This reasoning could also be justified by the fact that the US

---

[43] Also see, *ACLU v. Clapper* (Docket No. 14-4-cv, 2015), where NSA mass surveillance practices were ruled illegal.

[44] Kim L. Scheppele 'Law in a Time of Emergency: States of Exception and the Temptations of 9/11' (2004) 6 U. Pa. J. Const. L. 1001, 1059-1062, 1070-1071.

[45] E. Macaskill and G. Dance, 'NSA files: Decoded. What the revelations mean for you' (*The Guardian,* 1 November 2013). <http://www.theguardian.com/world/interactive/2013/nov/01/snowden-nsa-files-surveillance-revelations-decoded#section/1 > accessed 12 October 2015.

[46] Ibid.

has not experienced such a horrendous incident since 2001 and, very possibly, it could be for the unwillingness of some liberal-minded governments in Europe to impose similar, exceptional measures that the London bombings in 2005[47] and terrorist attacks at *Charlie Hebdo*[48] and in Copenhagen in 2015 happened.

The definitional and conceptual complexity of 'terrorism' creates 'a wider and wider sphere of potential dangers with smaller and smaller evidentiary base for each expansion of the threat'.[49] In the case of the US, the growing discriminating culture, that these measures create, results to 'a state that no longer provides Americans with dreams; instead, it has been reduced largely to protecting its citizens from a range of possible nightmares'.[50] As a result, we are witnessing Parliaments which exercise a loose and fitful oversight, Courts which intervene, although not truly decisively, only to condemn the most flagrant violations of constitutions and, with their active acquiescence, an almighty executive branch which imposes its orders without any serious constrains. As Benjamin Franklin once said, 'People willing to trade their freedom for temporary security deserve neither and will lose both'[51] and, interestingly enough, the public opinion has been sceptical over the years regarding balancing these two competing rights. Particularly, right after 9/11, the majority of Americans 'worried that the government wouldn't go far enough to monitor the activities of potential terrorists' but after the public outrage caused by the Snowden revelations in 2013 about government-conducted mass surveillance, the public 'was more worried about the government violating privacy rights'.[52] However, after the attacks in Paris and Copenhagen earlier this year and the continuous provocativeness of the so-called Islamic State, one could very plausibly argue that the public opinion is ready again to justify and accept additional executive measures restricting people's freedoms to enhance our national security. The challenging part of this process, though, is that this decision should not be made by state officials or intelligence agents behind closed doors without public debate. This decision should belong in a considerable extent to the public, using the

---

47 A series of additional legislation followed; see further above on page 121.

48 French intelligence had stopped monitoring the attackers although they had been previously convicted of terrorism, see Jamie Doward, 'Charlie Hebdo: could security services have prevented Paris attacks?' (*The Guardian* 10 January 2015) < http://www.theguardian.com/world/2015/jan/10/charlie-hebdo-security-services-paris-attacks > accessed 27 October 2015.

49 Scheppele, 1021.

50 Henry A. Giroux, 'Violence, Katrina and the Biopolitics of Disposability' (2007) 24 Theory, Culture & Society 305.

51 Benjamin Franklin, *Poor Richard' s Almanack* (1759).

52 D. Crumm, 'America 2015: Freedom or Security?' (*Read the Spirit*, January 2015) < http://www.readthespirit.com/ourvalues/america-2015-freedom-security/ > accessed 25 October 2015.

legislative and judicial safeguards available to us, to shield the fundamental principles of transparency, human rights, democracy and the rule of law established in the modern civilised world.

History has shown that Schmitt's idea of prolonged, exceptional measures leads, inevitably, to the establishment of totalitarian regimes. The rise of fascism, the experience of communism, the destruction of democratic governments and periods of total wars should be examples to avoid, whereas recently established constitutions, such as the South African Constitution, the 1993 Russian Constitution and the current German Constitution, which provide strong protection of human rights and guarantee strong safeguards, checks and balances during a state of exception, should be the real paradigm of contemporary politics.

6. Conclusion

Schmitt's idea of state of exception finds application by sovereign governments which, availing themselves of situations of crisis, go beyond their powers in the name of national security and public interest. Agamben has later analysed and further developed this theory, demonstrating that the use of exceptional powers to meet exceptional situations has now become the rule, rather than the exception, and defines contemporary politics, with the most recent examples to be found in the post-9/11 era. As the jurisprudence in the light of those events has shown, the prolonged state of emergency has been proved capable of providing the necessary legal basis for justifying any potential transgression of the law. The series of outrageous attacks against innocent civilians that has taken place in other Western countries since 11 September can resemble attacks against humanity and the universal values that civilised nations share. Yet, the greatest challenge for governments remains to strike the right balance between competing interests at stake, while making available sufficient judicial safeguards to ensure that the rule of law and democratic values are still protected.

The necessity, yet alone the legality, of these exceptional measures imposed in a state of exception will be always criticised; if not by the legislature or the judiciary, inevitably by the public. History, nevertheless, has taught that exceptional circumstances of necessity should not be seen 'as a moment when the rule of law should be suspended, but precisely a moment when the rule of law needs to be strengthened'.[53]

[53] Scheppele, 1003.

7. BIBLIOGRAPHY

Secondary Sources

Agamben G. *The State of Exception* (University of Chicago, 2005)

Agamben, G. 'The State of Exception', lecture at European Graduate School, 2003 http://www.egs.edu/faculty/giorgio-agamben/articles/the-state-of-exception/ .

America 2015: Freedom or Security?' < http://www.readthespirit.com/ourvalues/america-2015-freedom-security/ > accessed 25 October 2015.

Amnesty International France, Conference with Edward Snowden for Amnesty International France 10/12/2014 https://www.youtube.com/watch?v=nVRIVihRJuk [accessed on 13th April 2015].

Barack Obama, National Defence University speech on Counterterrorism, 2013, *New York Times,* May 23: http://www.nytimes.com/video/us/politics/100000002242352/president-obama-on-counterterrorism.html [accessed on 11th April 2015].

Chamayou, G. *A Theory of the Drone* (New Press 2015).

Cornwell, R. '9/11 lost decade: The American dream and the missing years', (*The Independent*, September 11 2011) < http://www.independent.co.uk/news/world/americas/911-lost-decade-the-american-dream-and-the-missing-years-2352870.html > accessed 19 October 2015.

Cratty C, 'FBI uses drones for surveillance in U.S', (*CNN*, June 20 2013) < http://edition.cnn.com/2013/06/19/politics/fbi-drones/ > accessed 19 October 2015.

De Benoist, A, Carl Schmitt. *Today: Terrorism, 'Just' War and the State of Emergency* (Arktos Media Ltd. 2013).

Fontana A, *Le droit de resistance: Du droit de resistance au devoir d'insurrection*. Jean-Claude Zancarini ed, Paris: ENS, 1999.

Giroux H. A, 'Violence, Katrina and the Biopolitics of Disposability' (2007) 24 *Theory, Culture & Society* 305.

Gross O, 'Chaos and rules: Should responses to violent crises always by constitutional?' (2011) Minnesota Public Law Research Paper No. 03-2, 1011.

Hamilton J, 'The delicate balance between civil liberties and national security' *(South African Judges Commission* 2006).

Hickman T. R, 'Between Human Rights and the Rule of Law: Indefinite detention and the derogation model of constitutionalism' (2005) 68 Modern Law Review 655.

http://leftfootforward.org/2011/09/ben-mitchell-how-the-9-11-response-changed-britain/ > accessed 24 October 2015.

Humphreys S, 'Legalising Lawlessness: On Giorgio Agamben's State of Exception' (2006) 17 *EJIL* 677.

Jason R, *America's War on Terror: The State of the 9/11 Exception from Bush to Obama* (Oxford, 2013).

Jenkins D, *The long decade: How 9/11 changed the law* (Oxford University Press, 2014).

Johns F, 'Guantanamo Bay and the Annihilation of the Exception', (2005) 16:4 European Journal of International Law 613.

Lye L, 'Easily Abused, Domestic drones raises enormous privacy concerns', (*American Civil Liberties Union*, 19 October 2012) < https://www.aclu.org/blog/speakeasy/easily-abused-domestic-drones-raise-enormous-privacy-concerns?redirect=blog/technology-and-liberty-national-security/easily-abused-domestic-drones-raise-enormous-privacy > accessed 23 October 2015.

Macaskill, E and Dance, G, 'NSA files: Decoded. What the revelations mean for you' (*The Guardian,* 1 November 2013) < http://www.theguardian.com/world/interactive/2013/nov/01/snowden-nsa-files-surveillance-revelations-decoded#section/1 > accessed 12 October 2015.

Masferrer D. A, *Post 9/11 and the State of Permanent Legal Emergency-Security and Human Rights in Countering Terrorism* (Springer, 2012).

Mitchell B, 'How the 9/11 response changed Britain' (*Left Foot Forward*, 11th September 2011).

Morgan M. J, *The impact of the 9/11 on Politics and War: The day that changed everything?* (Palgrave Macmillan, 2009).

Neocleous M, 'The Problem with Normality: Taking Exception to "Permanent Emergency' " (2006) 31:2 *Alternatives* 191

Pohlman H. L, *Terrorism and the Constitution: The post-9/11 cases* (Rowman & Littlefield Publishers 2008)

Reinach T, *De l'état de siège: Etudie Historique Et Juridique* (Kessinger Publishing, 2010),

Risen J and Lichtblau E, 'Bush Lets U.S. Spy on Callers Without Courts' (*The New York Times*, 16 December 2005) < http://www.nytimes.com/2005/12/16/politics/16program.html?pagewanted=all&_r=1& > accessed 23 October 2015.

Russell B, 'The battle for civil liberties: Government on offensive after criticism of 'authoritarian' laws' (*The Independent*, 17 April 2012) < http://www.independent.co.uk/news/uk/politics/the-battle-for-civil-liberties-government-on-offensive-after-criticism-of-authoritarian-laws-359794.html > accessed 24 October 2015.

Scheppele K. L, 'Law in a Time of Emergency: States of Exception and the Temptations of 9/11' (2004) 6 U. *Pa. J. Const. L.* 1001.
Schmitt C, *Political Theology* (MIT Press, 1985).
Schmitt C, *The concept of the Political* (University of Chicago 1996)
Snowden E, 'If I end up in Guantanamo, I can live with that' (*The Guardian Interviews*, 18 July 2014) < https://www.youtube.com/watch?v=L_amBkYx_Fk > accessed 23 October 2015.

US Legislation and Executive Measures

Authorization for Use of Military Force (AUMF) Act of 2001, 115 Stat. 224, US Congress S.J.Res. 23
Detainee Treatment Act of 2005
Military Order of 2001
USA Patriot Act of 2001
US Declaration of National Emergency, September 14, 2001, Proclamation 7463
US Renewal of the Declaration of Emergency, September 10, 2010
US Constitution

US Case Law

Rasul v. Bush U.S. 466 (2004)
Hamdi v. Rumsfeld 542 U.S. 507 (2004)
ACLU v. Clapper 14-42 (2015)

UK legislation

Anti-Terrorism, Crime and Security Act 2001
Counter-Terrorism Act 2008
Human Rights Act 1998
Prevention of Terrorism Act 2005
Terrorism Act 2000
Terrorism Act 2006

UK Case Law

A. v. Secretary of State for the Home Department [2004] UKHL 56
A v Secretary of State for the Home Department [2005] AC 68
X v Secretary of State for the Home Department [2005] AC 68

International Legislation

American Convention on Human Rights 1969
European Convention on Human Rights (ECHR) 1950
Geneva Convention on Prisoners of war 1929
International Covenant on Civil and Political Rights 1966

International Case Law

Lawless v. Ireland (No.3) (App.332/57) 1961
Ireland v. UK (App.5310/71) 1978

Omissions and the Mysterious Public Veil: Consideration of the "Immunity" of Public Authorities in Negligence Claims

Jason Yong[†]

The law of omissions regarding emergency services have always been rather controversial because of the vague 'public immunity' defence or justification invoked by the courts. In light of the recent decisions by the highest courts regarding the emergency services, including the latest Supreme Court decisions of Smith v Ministry of Defence[1] *and Michael v Chief Constable of South Wales*[2]*, this article questions whether the logical underpinnings of the defence itself is prima facie reasonable. This article questions further whether the same judicial reasoning for omissions should be applied to the general public and emergency services, given that the latter do occupy a position above the general layman and is able to actively prevent harm from being inflicted onto the claimants.*

Keywords: Tort Law; Negligence; Omissions; Public Authorities; Immunity; Hill v CC of West Yorkshire; Michael v Chief Constable of South Wales.

1. Introduction

In *Yuen Kun Yeu v A-G of Hong Kong*, Lord Keith famously stated that it would be quite preposterous to impose 'liability in negligence on the part of

---

[†] LLB (Hons.), King's College London.

[1] [2014] AC 52.

[2] [2015] UKSC 2.

one who sees another about to walk off a cliff with his head in the air and forbears to shout a warning'.[3] In short, while society does encourage kind and selfless behaviour to help others, the law does not punish those who had the opportunity but have chosen not to become 'good Samaritans'. In fact, it does not make much sense to impose such liability anyway. Lord Hoffmann, in *Stovin v Wise*, stated that it would be unreasonable if such a duty to prevent harm to others existed, as an innumerate group of people would become liable for each harm suffered.[4]

While that rationale is reasonable when applied to defendants belonging to the general public, this article questions whether that reasoning can subsist when applied to the context of emergency services and the armed forces. In doing so, this article will briefly explore the aims of tort law itself before examining whether the genesis and development of the 'public immunity' reasoning remains justifiable and logical today. Following which, this article will analyse the latest Supreme Court decisions, such as *Smith v Ministry of Defence*[5] and *Michael v Chief Constable of South Wales*[6], and raises pertinent questions pertaining to the judicial reasoning behind the courts' decisions in denying liability on emergency services and the armed forces, when they *could have* actively prevented harm from occurring because they were furnished with more resources and information than the average layman, but had failed to do so.

2. Main Aims of Tort

Lord Dyson, in *Jones v Kaney*[7], explains that the entire system of law predicates on the fundamental notion of addressing wrongful behaviour. A wrong, in the context of tort law, is simply a breach of a duty owed to someone else which results in harm to another. Harm refers to any physical or mental damage, or a material and tangible detriment or loss to a person. Without a system that lies on such a 'cornerstone' of justice, the public perception of the law as an infallible system of fairness and impartiality would be severely undermined.[8] The law, therefore, takes a much stricter stance on imposing liability on the wrongdoer, and providing a remedy to the victim.

There are a few popular theories of tort. While they differ slightly on what is the ultimate goal that the system of tort law achieves, they agree on the fundamental concept that harms which result from another's wrongdoing

---

[3] [1988] AC 175, 192.
[4] [1996] AC 923, 944.
[5] *Smith, supra.*
[6] *Michael, supra.*
[7] [2011] 2 AC 398.
[8] Ibid., 113.

should be remedied by law. Some writers believe that tort law provides a structure that provides compensation for harms caused. Lord Dyson, writing extra-judicially this time, argues that if a party has harmed another through foreseeable actions, and there is a sufficient degree of proximity between the two parties, the wrongdoer should compensate the victim.[9] In doing so, the compensation model provides an element of deterrence; there is an economic disincentive for people to commit the same wrongs. On the other hand, several writers believe that tort law is just about righting a wrong between two parties. Weinrib highlights the exclusive nature of the relationship between the party which inflicted harm and the victim and argues that tort law is only about the imposition of liability on one party and the distribution of remedies to the other.[10] Stevens, however, believes that wrongs in tort law are defined so because everybody has an inherent right not to be treated in a certain manner.[11] However, the fundamental point of agreement is that tort law does provide a structure to remedy such wrongs, and especially harm, which occur in society.

3. THE GENESIS OF THE 'IMMUNITY' OF PUBLIC AUTHORITIES

However, the courts have always relied on a controversial line of reasoning when public authorities, including emergency services and armed forces, are sued for negligence, and that is of the defence of public 'immunity'. The source of this infamous controversy arose from *Hill v CC of West Yorkshire*[12], which involved the murder of a young woman by the 'Yorkshire Ripper'. There were two strands of reasoning from Lord Keith's decision to not hold the police liable for failing to save the deceased. Firstly, unlike *Home Office v Dorset Yacht*[13], there was no special relationship between the police and the deceased. It cannot be said that there is sufficient legal proximity between the police and a potential victim of a crime.[14] Secondly, as a matter of public policy, the police are immune from actions for negligence. Imposing liability for negligence would result in the police acting defensively, and that would adversely affect the effectiveness of the police when they carry out

[9] Lord Dyson MR, 'The Duty of Care of Public Authorities: Too Much, Too Little or About Right?' (PIBA Richard Davies Lecture, London, November 2012), 3.
[10] Ernest J. Weinrib, *The Idea of Private Law* (Harvard University Press, New York City, 1995), 1.
[11] R Stevens, *Torts and Rights* (Oxford University Press, London, 2007), 2.
[12] [1988] 2 WLR 1049.
[13] [1970] AC 1004.
[14] *Hill*, 62.

investigation and supress crime.[15] Henceforth, the *Hill* 'immunity' shall refer to Lord Keith's second strand of reasoning.

Nonetheless, this 'immunity' is qualified and only applies for cases regarding omissions; the police continue to remain liable for negligence if harm was directly caused or contributed by their actions. For example, in *Informer v Chief Constable*, the Court held that the police owed a duty of care to the claimant because they had recruited him as a covert human intelligence source; by placing him in a position of risk, the law dictates that the police cannot deny their responsibility for the claimant's physical safety and well-being.[16]

3.1. Development of the 'Immunity' of Public Authorities

However, the greatest problem with the *Hill* 'immunity' principle was the way in which the court applied the principle outside of the facts present in *Hill.* The original case concerned two blameworthy parties: the Yorkshire Ripper and the negligent police force. McIvor makes a salient point: *Hill* was a unique case concerning third party liability, which is a unique species within the law of omissions liability. In such cases, the courts are slow to impose liability of negligence on the middleman because there was always a more blameworthy party, i.e. the third party.[17] In *Caparo v Dickman*, Lord Bridge emphasised the principle that the law of negligence should develop incrementally. When considering cases with different facts, the courts should be careful to apply rules from previous analogous cases.[18] However, this sort of judicial scrutiny was lacking in two cases which has effectively expanded the ambit of the *Hill* principle. In *X v Bedfordshire CC*, when Lord Browne-Wilkinson endorsed the *Hill* reasoning and extended the 'immunity' of the police forces to 'all those charged by Parliament with the task of protecting others'.[19] This means that the ambit of the principle has been expanded to include *all* public authorities, including emergency services and the armed forces. Again, in *Brooks v Commissioner of Police of the Metropolis*[20], which concerned the negligence of the police during a racist attack on the claimant, the court merely applied the *Hill* principle. In both cases, the House of Lords merely applied the *Hill* principle without considering the individual factual contexts, and failed to provide cogent justification why the *Hill* principle

---

[15] Ibid., 63.
[16] [2012] 3 All ER 601.
[17] Claire McIvor, 'Getting defensive about police negligence: the Hill principle, the Human Rights Act 1998 and the House of Lords' [2010] CLJ 133, 141.
[18] [1990] 2 AC 605, 618.
[19] [1995] 2 AC 633, 751.
[20] [2005] 1 WLR 1495.

should extend outside third party liability situations. It is argued that this broad-brush approach adopted in both cases, in contradistinction to the scrutiny advocated in *Caparo*, in failing to take into account the unique factual situation in *Hill* is strong indication that the public 'immunity' should not be blindly applied in all negligence cases concerning public authorities today.

In addition to arguing that the extension of the *Hill* principle outside third party liability situations was questionable, the following parts in the article will argue that the underlying justification for the principle itself is flawed. Further, if the principle of defensive practice cannot subsist as a reasonable argument, then there should be reason to redefine the limits of the 'conflict of duties' defence.

3.2. The 'Defensive Practice' Argument Is Flawed

A strong indication of the fallibility of the 'defensive practice' argument is that this policy consideration has not been consistently applied through case law. In *Dorset Yacht*, Lord Reid explicitly denied the existence of such fears of the suppression of police efficiency in the presence of legal duties.[21] This argument was denied again in *Phelps v Hillingdon LBC*, where Lord Clyde was doubtful that such an attitude of fearful defensive practice will exist in real life.[22] In *Barrett v Enfield LBC*, the contrary was even suggested; the potential existence of liability would actually enhance the overall standard among public authority employees.[23] Perhaps the reason for the court's inconsistency lies in the fact that the defensive practice argument is very conjectural in nature. Fairgrieve, in a case commentary of *Smith v MOD* (analysis below), points out that the defence is premised on 'anecdote and assumption', and there is no empirical evidence to suggest that there would be a culture of defensive practice.[24] There is a strong reason for agreeing with the conclusion drawn by Fairgrieve; in *Hill*, Lord Keith merely pointed to the *possibility* that the police might act defensive if liability was imposed on them[25], and there have been no following cases which lists out evidence that the imposition of liability *will* generate a culture of defensive practice. Additionally, the defensive practice argument has been denied in Canada. In *Hill v Hamilton-Wentworth Regional Police Services Board*, the Canadian

---

[21] *Dorset Yacht*, 1033.
[22] [2001] 2 AC 619, 672.
[23] [2001] 2 AC 550, 568.
[24] Duncan Fairgrieve, 'Suing the military: the justiciability of damages claims against the armed forces', [2014] CLJ 18, 20.
[25] *Hill*.

courts refused to recognise an investigatory immunity for the police, explicitly ruling out that there would be a culture of defensive practice.[26]

There is a further problem with the application of the defensive practice argument. In the latest decisions concerning the emergency services and the armed forces, it seems like the defensive practice mentality has taken such prevalence in the minds of the highest courts that they dismiss any cases of negligence concerning public authorities without analysing each case for its merits. This has led to conflicting decisions between the Court of Appeal, the House of Lords and the Supreme Court.

In the Court of Appeal decision of *Smith v Chief Constable of Sussex Police*[27], the court followed the earlier decision of *Swinney v Chief Constable of Northumbria*[28] and argued that, in contrast to the claimant in *Hill*, Smith's claim did not depend on his status as a member of the general public facing a common risk; rather, because he was a witness for the police, an analogous position to those occupied by informants, he should be entitled to a measure of protection.[29] However, when the case was considered again in the combined appeal of *Van Colle v Chief Constable of Hertfordshire*, the House of Lords adopted a blunt utilitarian rationale and dismissed the appeal on the basis that the defensive practice argument effective overwrote any claim against the police for negligence, regardless of the status of the claimant.[30] While applying the *Hill* principle, several of their Lordships mentioned *obiter* that they were bound by precedent to deny any liability on the part of the police, but noted their dissatisfaction with the outcome by stating that the law was in need of reform.[31]

In the recent armed forces decision of *Smith v MOD*[32], the judicial confusion about the correct weight of the *Hill* principle was readily apparent in the close 4:3 decision of the Supreme Court. Lord Hope, representing the majority, stated that the general source of public 'immunity' from *Hill* has been extended and applied to situations involving the armed forces in *Mulcahy v MOD*[33]. However, a decent proportion of his Lordship's judgment was dedicated to proving that the scope of 'combat immunity', a relative of the *Hill* 'immunity' principle, should be curtailed to include only actions taken in the course of actual or imminent armed conflict.[34] It is for that reason that the *Challenger* claims could be permitted because they concerned a

---

[26] (2007) 285 DLR (4th) 620.
[27] [2008] EWCA Civ 39.
[28] [1997] Q.B. 464.
[29] *Smith v Chief Constable of Sussex Police*, 29.
[30] [2009] 1 A.C. 225, 75.
[31] Ibid., 102, per Lord Phillips. See also, 107, per Lord Carswell.
[32] *Smith*.
[33] [1996] QB 732, 750.
[34] *Smith*, 92.

preparatory stage in the operations, whereas the *Ellis* claims concerned a phase where there was an imminent threat of war.[35] Lord Mance, one of the dissenting judges, disagreed on this point. He argued that it was impossible to distinguish between decisions made during pre-combat preparation and decision made during actual combat.[36] Lord Mance's argument is logical; the entire operation of the armed forces when it is engaging in war is geared towards the goal of combat. It is arbitrary to draw lines between activities that are 'preparatory' and 'combat' in nature, because *all* activities seek to achieve the purpose of warfare.

Furthermore, Lords Mance and Carnwarth note the problem of giving the *Hill* principle too much weight relative to the other factors would result in a situation where the judges cannot see the wood for the trees, for doing so would be engaging in a 'dilemma'.[37] Lord Mance states that it is incorrect to determine common law liability based on the position which the defendant occupies and whether he falls within the ambit of the *Hill* principle, but rather the determination of liability involves the balancing exercise between the considerations of harm and any public policy considerations, one of which is combat immunity.[38] McIvor makes a similar point in her article regarding police liability: the courts are too preoccupied with the ambit of any public authority 'immunity', and will only consider a duty of care as an exception.[39] There is therefore strong authority to suggest that there too much judicial weight is given to the *Hill* principle. Even in the original case of *Hill v Chief Constable of West Yorkshire* itself, it was raised as a public policy exception to deny liability. The problematic arrangement of perceiving the *Hill* immunity as a *prima facie* assumption that *all* public authorities will not be liable for their negligence leads to decisions where the courts may fail to impose any duty on the individual merits of the case. Whilst Lord Rodger's statement that not all harms suffered can be remedied by law is correct, the heavy-handed utilitarian reasoning adopted by the courts, when giving the immunity a higher priority, is submitted to be an incorrect form of reasoning. Failure to appreciate the individual merits of the case *before* considering the exceptions is argued to be a betrayal of the first priority of the law to seek to rectify wrongs.

The correct approach was adopted in the latest Supreme Court decision of *Michael v Chief Constable of South Wales*.[40] Lord Toulson, representing the majority, was at pains to state that the denial of liability was not because of

---

[35] Ibid., 94–95.
[36] Ibid., 125.
[37] Ibid., 161.
[38] Ibid., 149.
[39] McIvor, 145.
[40] *Michael*.

the existence of police immunity[41], but rather because there was a lack of sufficient factual evidence to create an exception under the general omission principle.[42] It is argued that this approach is correct: the courts should only consider any public policy considerations only *after* the examination of the general law of omissions. However, Lord Toulson seems to suggest that previous decisions were recognised on this correct approach.[43] It is argued that this is a flawed proposition. The authorities analysed above which already prove that the court denied liability for public authorities because they considered the public 'immunity' as a rule, rather than as an exception. In addition, in *Kent v Griffiths*, liability was imposed on the ambulance services because their duties were thought to be equivalent of that to doctors and nurses, persons acting in a private capacity, and not that of the police and fire services.[44] In doing so, Lord Woolf implied that those occupying public office would *not* be found liable if they were found in a similar position because of the nature of their occupation. This is another salient example whereby the courts have denied liability because of the existence of public immunity.

3.3. The 'Conflict of Duties' Argument Should Take Into Consideration the Flawed 'Immunity' Principle

It is submitted that Lord Toulson's approach in *Michael* is correct: the default position under omissions liability is an absence of liability, but there should be a balancing exercise of policy factors to determine if an exception can be created to find liability, and one of the possible policy considerations is the public 'immunity' principle. However, as argued above, the 'immunity' principle is flawed *in substance*, and should therefore not be given much judicial weight. As a result, the balancing exercise should not always be skewed towards the denial of liability when considering cases concerning public bodies.

The 'conflict of duties' argument is a defence against the finding of liability on the basis that the action to save or protect the claimant and conflicts with the public duty of the defendant to protect a larger group of persons. In two of the three appeals in *Capital Counties v Hampshire County Council*, the Court of Appeal stated that the fire services were not liable for causing damage to the claimants' property because the process of extinguishing the fire included damage to neighbouring properties.[45] The

---

[41] Ibid., 116.
[42] Ibid., 115.
[43] Ibid.
[44] [2001] QB 36, 46.
[45] [1997] QB 1004, 1036.

recognition of the private duty of care would undermine the defendant authority's primary public duties to prevent fire damage to all properties.

The element that the recognition of the claimed duty of care will undermine another duty of care owed a larger group of people is key to the 'conflict of duties' argument. It follows that if the claimed duty of care *does not* conflict against another larger duty of care, the 'conflict of duties' will *not* be a reason to find an absence of liability. In addition, if the non-conflicting private duty of care owed to the claimant falls within one of the recognised exceptions to the omissions principle, it is logical that the defendant will owe the claimant a duty of care.

In *Kent v Griffiths*, the court held that the ambulance services were liable for the negligence of sending an ambulance on time. They stated that there is no conflict of duties between the claimant and the larger public. Rather, because only an identified individual called the emergency hotline, the only person who could be adversely affected for the failure of the ambulance services to respond on time is the dialler himself.[46]

However, both the Court of Appeal and Supreme Court denied liability for the police in the case of *Michael v Chief Constable of South Wales*. In that case, it was the failure of the police to respond on time to an emergency call which resulted in the tragic death of Miss Michael. Lord Toulson distinguished the case from *Kent v Griffiths* on the basis that the call handler in *Kent* had misled the deceased by assuring them that the ambulance would arrive shortly. On the other hand, this element of 'assurance' was absent in the facts of *Michael*. It was taken that the police had not assumed any responsibility for the lack of its actions against Michael, and therefore an exception cannot be created to impose liability on the negligence of the police.[47] It is submitted that this is an arbitrary distinction. Regardless whether it is the police, which are taken to occupy public office, or the ambulance service, which is perceived to be in the private sphere, the fact remains that both are emergency services that respond to calls from the public. It makes sense that people have a certain common perception that the emergency services will respond quickly. Potential victims call emergency hotlines in the most desperate time of need, and it often represents their lack of alternatives available to them. The reliance on emergency services represents all they can do to seek help. It would be unfair to the public if it the law recognises that the emergency services could effectively shirk off its duties to respond quickly by omitting any reassurances in its call.

---

46 *Kent*, 45.

47 *Michael*, 138.

3.4. The Liability Principle Can Be the Solution to the Existing Problem

In *Van Colle*, Lord Bingham attempted to create the 'liability principle' that addressed this apparent lacuna in the law. He wrote that if a specific member of the public were to give a public authority employee sufficient credible evidence that a third party was creating a specific and imminent threat to his life and physical safety, the public authority then owes that specific member of the public a duty to assess the threat, and if required, take reasonable steps to prevent the threat altogether.[48] However, the Supreme Court in *Van Colle*, and both the Court of Appeal and the Supreme Court in *Michael* refused to endorse the 'liability principle. Lord Toulson in *Michael* reiterates the objections to the principle from *Van Colle*, stating that the principle creates an unacceptable arbitrary distinction between people who call the emergency services, and others who do not. He goes further in stating that there are insufficient elements of a unique relationship between the caller and the emergency services encapsulated in the principle, therefore the failure to protect the claimant, which is part of its larger duty to society, does not automatically give rise to a private cause of action.[49]

It is argued that Lord Toulson's analysis was faulty in two respects. Firstly, Lord Kerr, representing the minority, presents a refined version of Lord Bingham's 'liability principle'; if a person delivered personalized information about an imminent attack to anyone, the police is said to owe a duty of care to that intended victim because they are furnished with specific information and therefore have the capability to prevent the attack. The quintessential element of specific and personalised information to the intended victim, to be found in the factual matrix of each case, is key to establishing the degree of proximity between the police and the victim, which was lacking in Lord Bingham's principle.[50] Lord Toulson dismisses this argument on the basis that the test for proximity is circular and provides no useful measurement for determining liability in law.[51] Lord Kerr concedes its circular nature, but the entire test for proximity, in of itself, is already circular, and yet it continues to be used by the courts today for the test of negligence. This is an indication that the circular test still retains utilitarian value for determining liability[52], so there should be no reason to dismiss Lord Kerr's refined 'liability principle' on this point.

Secondly, while Lord Toulson agreed with the underlying rationale of the 'liability principles' from the submissions and the minority, he argued that the proposition that acceptance of the principle would create an improvement in

---

[48] *Van Colle*, 44.

[49] *Michael*, 120; see also *Gorringe v Calderdale MBC* [2004] 1 WLR 1057.

[50] Ibid., 168.

[51] Ibid., 133.

[52] Ibid., 145–146.

the efficiency of public authorities is speculative at best. The only significant undesirable public policy eventuality which Lord Toulson proposes is that the police would suffer significant financial ramifications,[53] and this is submitted to be a flimsy defence for the argument for public authority liability in such situations. It may be the case that Lord Kerr's test will create arbitrary distinctions between people who dial the emergency hotline and people who do not, but this should not prevent the law from recognising liability on the police, or any public authority, where their blatant omissions have resulted in tragic, but entirely avoidable, consequences.[54] When authorities have been furnished with specific information, and therefore could have done something to prevent the harm, it seems ironic that the law is bound by its own rules and is unable to provide a remedy.[55] The salient point must be reiterated: when the caller has done all he can to furnish information to the emergency services to prevent the occurrence of harm during a desperate time, it seems unfair that the authorities will not be found liable for their negligence simply because they have not done anything. They occupy a specific role in society which carries the common perception that they will respond in urgent situations, however the law only attaches liability when the authorities 'reassures' the caller. In other situations, they would not be found liable. This is an unacceptable state of judicial reasoning.

4. THE ALTERNATIVE ACTION UNDER HRA 1998

Under the Human Rights Act 1998 (HRA 1998), individuals can rely on specific rights under the European Convention in litigation against other legal entities, including public authorities. In the latest decisions concerning the emergency services and the armed forces, the common law claim for negligence was always tried in conjunction with an Article 2 ECHR claim, which concerns the right to life. Therefore, the question is whether the common law action in negligence should develop in tandem the statutory action for breach of ECHR rights under HRA 1998. This is especially so since section 2 HRA 1998 states that the courts cannot act incompatibly with the Convention or the jurisprudence from the European Court of Human Rights.

While *Osman v UK* is commonly remembered for the Strasbourg court's misunderstanding of the English law of negligence, its test for the liability of public authorities remains important: in third party liability situations, there should be a factual inquiry to determine if the authorities had known of a real

[53] Ibid., 121–122.
[54] Ibid., 171.
[55] S. Tofaris and S. Steel, "Police Liability in Negligence for Failure to Prevent Crime: Time to Rethink" (University of Cambridge Legal Studies Research Paper Series, Paper No 39/2014).

and immediate threat, and whether they could have reasonably been expected to prevent that risk.[56] This presented a new and distinct test of liability from the common law of negligence. However, the Supreme Court in *Van Colle* was determined to emphasise that the findings under common law will not be undone by any claims under HRA 1998, thereby implying that there are two distinct tests for the law of negligence.[57] McIvor writes that the result of this is that subsequent cases would usually fail for both claims.[58] It is argued that her reaction was rather excessive: it is plain from the latest decisions of *Smith* and *Michael*, that the HRA claims have succeeded when the common law claims were dismissed.

Lady Hale, in the minority in *Michael*, argued for the proposition that the common law duties for public authorities *should* develop in tandem with the obligations of public bodies under HRA 1998. Lord Toulson, however, rejects this call for pro-harmonization between the two distinct causes of actions because of the different rationales giving rise to each action.[59] It is argued that Lord Toulson's approach of differentiating the two tests of liability makes sense. The entire bases of the two types of laws are already different; the common law has a duty to remedy wrongs, whereas Convention claims are intended to maintain the minimum standard of basic freedoms. There is, therefore, no sound reason for creating a single test for two distinctly different kinds of claims.

Lord Toulson is correct that any form of reform in this area of law, whether to address the questionable weight of the 'immunity' principle or to collate the two tests for liability, should be left to the decision of Parliament.[60] It is not for the common law to determine it on its own accord without introducing a host of uncertain rules through extensive jurisprudence and different interpretations by different judges. Most importantly, interference by the common law runs the risk of infringing the sanctity offered by the separation of legislative and judiciary powers.

However, it seems that all hopes of leaving reform in the hands of the Government may be futile. In 2008, the Law Commission published a Consultation Paper detailing that the underlying rationale of the tort of negligence to 'provide compensation for those who suffer loss as a result of the negligence of others' should apply equally regardless whether the defendant is a public individual or private body.[61] Unfortunately, in a subsequent paper published in May 2010, the Law Commission announced its

---

[56] [1998] EHRR 101, 116.
[57] *Van Colle*.
[58] McIvor, 146.
[59] *Michael*, 127.
[60] Ibid., 130.
[61] Law Commission, *Administrative Redress: Public Bodies and the Citizen* (Law Com CP No 187, 2008).

intentions to abandon any reform efforts in this area of law because 'the key stakeholder – Government – was firmly opposed' to its recommendations.[62] In *Mohammed v Home Office*, Sedley LJ commented directly on this episode and stated: 'it is a troubling comment on the functioning of the separation of powers that the state's independent law reform advisory body has had to abandon a project affecting the liability of government to govern principally because the control exercised by government over Parliament would frustrate any reform, however wise or necessary, which would make government's life more difficult'.[63] It is an unfortunate and lamentable reality that any reform proposed by the Law Commission or within this article itself would not be implemented in the foreseeable future.

5. Conclusion

This article is not intended to pin blame on those who willingly join the civil service in the noble pursuit of protecting and saving lives. For example, it would be blatantly unfair and unreasonable to impose liability on hospitals if patients pass away due to natural causes. However, this article attempts to point out that in certain cases whereby it is clear that the public authority in question has fallen short of its mandatory operating protocol, which leads to the harm or death of innocent individuals who have called for their help, the courts tend to obfuscate the judicial process of determining their liability. In other words, it has been highlighted in this article that the courts have failed to distinguish between situations where harm and death is not of the fault of the public authorities, and other situations where their blatant omissions have caused the harm and death of innocent individuals. It is argued that the fact that public authorities have, for an uncomfortable period of time, been given a blanket immunity which manifests great social injustice. The result in *Michael v Chief Constable of South Wales*[64] is just one of the many decisions which illustrate the awkward jurisprudence of not having any authority to account for their mistakes. It is argued that it is incorrect to attach judicial weight to a principle, and consequently deny any liability, on the speculative basis that the public bodies *might* drop in efficiency in the future. This article recognises the efforts of our everyday heroes which often go unnoticed, but the law should not forget that these heroes are also mortals which err. The point which this articles tries to emphasise is this: if society cannot rely on the public

[62] Law Commission, *Administrative Redress: Public Bodies and the Citizen* (Law Com No 322, 2010), paras 1.3 and 1.6.
[63] [2011] 1 WLR 2862, 23.
[64] *Michael*.

authorities for responding promptly at its most crucial juncture, who else can society turn to in its most dire time of need?

Legal Issues is operated by volunteers and relies on donations.
To support the Journal or UKLSA in general, email president@uklsa.co.uk.

If you are interested in joining the editorial board as an editor, reviewer, copy-editor, or formatting editor, email editor@uklsa.co.uk

Website: http://www.uklsa.co.uk
Facebook: https://www.facebook.com/UKLSA
Twitter: https://twitter.com/UKLSA

www.ingramcontent.com/pod-product-compliance
Lightning Source LLC
LaVergne TN
LVHW082344200926
848481LV00012B/3444
* 9 7 9 8 2 1 5 1 9 1 7 9 8 *